FASCINATING FACTS FOR
CURIOUS KIDS

1001 Amazing and Mind-Blowing Kid Friendly Facts About Science, History, and the World We Live In

I0116729

INCLUDES 99 TRIVIA QUESTIONS!

PROFESSOR PRODIGY

Published by Professor Prodigy

ISBN: 979-8-9898785-6-7

UNLOCK A WORLD OF WONDERS!

Step into a world of wonders with Professor Prodigy's digital adventure kit - Where Learning Meets Adventure!

Step into Professor Prodigy's World of Wonders!

Fun Fact: It's FREE!

Prepare to embark on an exhilarating adventure filled with fascinating facts, hands-on experiments, and imaginative challenges. From crafting your very own nature collage to unveiling the secrets of ancient history, Professor Prodigy's 'World Of Wonders' is your portal to a treasure trove of knowledge and excitement.

For a limited time, you'll also have the chance to win personalized and exclusive puppet content!

Scan the QR code now to enter and to claim your free download. Embark on this remarkable journey with Professor Prodigy today!

Grab Your Copy Now!

JOIN US ON SOCIAL MEDIA

SCAN ME

Follow Professor Prodigy's Adventures on Social Media!

Wanna follow more of Professor Prodigy's adventures? Just scan the QR code to join 'Professor Prodigy's Pals' – our FREE Facebook community.

As a member, you'll enjoy a plethora of exclusive perks, including:
- Puppet shows and opportunities for personalized puppet content.
- Adventurous and engaging worksheets.
- A place to showcase your prodigy's masterpieces.
- Exclusive sneak peeks of our upcoming books and other exciting projects.
- A treasure trove of free printables.
- Announcements about Professor Prodigy's global travels.
...and so much more!

Connect with parents of fellow explorers, share your kiddo's discoveries, and become part of a community that is passionately dedicated to the never-ending quest for knowledge. Let's make every day an adventure!

WE LOVE HEARING FROM YOU!

Your feedback is precious to us! If you've enjoyed our book, please consider leaving us a review. As a dedicated team of moms and a passionate graphic designer, we strive for accuracy and fun in every fact that we share. However, we're only human, and sometimes errors slip through.

- **For Fact Corrections:** If you notice any inaccuracies in the content of our book, please let us know at hello@professorprodigy.com. We're committed to fixing it and ensuring the best experience for all curious minds.

- **For Printing Issues:** Please note that our printing and shipping is handled by Amazon directly, and any physical printing errors are beyond our control. If you encounter such issues, we are so sorry. Please kindly contact Amazon Customer Service for assistance.

Your understanding and support helps us improve and enables us to continue to bring engaging and accurate content to our young readers!

★ ★ ★ ★ ★

This book is lovingly dedicated to my daughters, Makenna and Caitlyn, who fill my life with joy and inspiration. To my niece and nephews whose curiosity propels me forward. To Rye, whose enthusiasm for Professor Prodigy has been unwavering from the very start. And last but most certainly not least, to my love, whose belief in me and love for me has been my guiding light, even in moments when I doubted myself.

OUR ADVENTURE BEGINS

Greetings, explorer! I'm Professor Prodigy, your guide into the fantastical world of facts! This book is the first of many to chronicle my journeys around the world, through time, and back again. As you adventure with me through each fact I hope that you will let them spark your curiosity and inspire your imagination. So, get ready to head to the land of the gross and gruesome, dive into the weird and the wonderful, and venture into the realm of the astonishing!

Are you ready to meet creatures that can produce gallons of slime to deter their predators? Or maybe you're most curious about how some creatures can regrow their body parts (even you)? Perhaps you're most excited to step into the labyrinth of bizarre scientific discoveries that have shaped our understanding of the universe? If that sounds like you then grab your lab coats, adjust your goggles, and let's delve into this treasure trove of fascinating facts. Oh, I'm so excited! There's no adventure more exciting than the quest for knowledge!

Let's go!

Professor Prodigy's Packing List

Compass

Microscope

Rain Boots

Notebook and Pencils

Binoculars

Pocket-Sized Shrink Ray

Flashlight

World Map

Time Travel Stopwatch

Sun Hat

Reusable Water Bottle

Snacks

Invisibility Cloak

CREATURE FEATURES: MARVELS & MYSTERIES

1. Hold onto your spectacles, future Einsteins! Here comes the hagfish. Found in the cold depths of the ocean, these slippery survivors can conjure a storm of slime when threatened, swelling up to 10,000 times their size! Despite having no jaws or bones, their unique adaptations have allowed them to thrive and swim around the earth for over 300 million years.

2. Delving deep under the sea, we find the blobfish. These guys live in the deep trenches of the ocean, where the water pressure helps give their bodies shape. Once they reach the surface and the pressure is gone, their bodies become squishy and gooey, giving them a rather grumpy appearance. Don't judge a fish by its frown!

3. Hoot hoot! The Eastern screech owl from North America is a master of disguise. It can camouflage seamlessly with plumage that perfectly matches tree bark. This owl can be found in two color morphs, gray and red, to match different types of trees. A wise and unseen creature of the night!

4. Walking in the tropical forests of Southeast Asia, the walking leaf insect is nature's masterpiece. This insect's body, legs, and even wings are shaped like leaves, with veins and brown spots, making it almost indistinguishable from lifelike foliage. It's one of nature's most unique disguises!

5. Watch out for the slime! We are about to discover the resilient triton snail, a marine wonder able to regenerate its shell and internal organs! Specialized cells called blastemal cells kick into action, allowing the snail to regrow lost tissues!

6. Hidden in Southeast Asia's rainforests, the violin beetle serenades silently. Its body, shaped like the instrument, helps it to wedge into tight spaces, protecting it from predators. And here's a fun fact: its unique shape also aids in camouflage, making it look like a part of the wood it's on. The forest's very own stringed maestro!

7. Next, we encounter the ant-mimicking jumping spider. It has perfected the art of mimicry. It looks like an ant and mimics their movements, swaying side to side as it walks, deceiving predators and avoiding becoming a tasty treat for birds. The ultimate game of hide and seek, spider edition!

8. African bullfrogs produce toxic mucus to deter predators. This mucus has a lot of jobs! It keeps the frog moist and free from bacteria. During dry spells, they use this mucus and shed skin to create a cocoon, helping them survive harsh conditions. Talk about a survival hack!

9. Hop in our time machine and rewind to the days of the silverfish. This ancient insect has been thriving for over 400 million years and is a master of survival. With its carrot-shaped body and bristly tail, it's a living relic that's been around since even before the dinosaurs. A relic from the past, still sneaking around today!

10. Scuba gear on! Let's swim with the cleaner shrimp. The small but mighty regenerators of the sea! Lose a limb? They can regrow it during the next molting cycle, returning to full functionality. It's a shrimp-tacular tale of resilience and renewal in the aquatic world!

11. Next, we come across the velvet ant. But don't let its velvety, soft appearance fool you; its sting is as fierce as its fuzz is soft. And here's a tidbit: despite its name, it's not an ant at all! It's actually a wingless female wasp. A deceptive beauty with a bite!

12. Soaring over to the dense woodlands of Asia, the lanternfly displays its beautiful and intricate wing patterns. This insect uses its vibrant colors to help it blend seamlessly into tree bark, evading keen-eyed predators like birds. Asia's hidden gem, fluttering in plain sight!

13. Grab your snorkels, and let's dive into the mystical waters of Mexico to meet the axolotl. This unique salamander is neotenic, which means, unlike other salamanders, they do not complete metamorphosis and live entirely in water. How do they manage to live underwater and stay looking young? Their slippery skin serves as their lungs, extracting oxygen directly from water. Who said growing up was necessary?

14. As night blankets Asia, the atlas moth emerges. This giant, one of the largest moths in the world, has wingtips that mimic snake heads. This mimicry deters potential predators, making them think twice before approaching. It's the night's most enchanting flyer, with a touch of intimidation!

15. If you prefer a creature that lives up to its name, meet the ghost slug. Found in the woodlands of Wales, its pale and slimy appearance, devoid of eyes or shell, is haunting. This slug uses its slime to glide through the soil, hunting down earthworms to eat with its razor-sharp teeth.

16. Back on land, earthworms have found a slick solution to tunneling. Their slimy mucus helps them slide through the soil while breathing through their skin. As they wiggle, they also make the soil healthier. Indeed, they are the slimy superheroes of the garden!

17. Soaring in next are the harpy eagles. Native to the tropical rainforests of Central and South America, these powerful raptors have sticky pads on their feet to snatch prey mid-flight. With the strength to take down monkeys and sloths, they're one of the world's fiercest birds.

18. Mud boots on, adventurers, as we explore our own backyards! Let's wriggle through the soil with the earthworms, the masters of regeneration! Depending on the species, they can regrow an entire head, tail, or even smaller body portions. A squiggly tale of resilience and renewal beneath the ground!

19. Down under in Australia, the tawny frogmouth plays a game of "I'm not here!" By day, it perches on branches, stretching its body to mimic a tree branch. When night falls, this nocturnal bird becomes active, hunting for its prey. The ultimate peekaboo predator!

20. Climb aboard our fascination ferry and float with the tiny but mighty freshwater hydra! This aquatic invertebrate can regrow its entire body, even if cut into tiny pieces! A dicey tale of regrowth beneath the waves!

21. Let's venture deeper into the tropics of Central and South America, where the tailless whip scorpion is on the prowl. Those whip-like front legs, covered in tiny hairs, can detect vibrations, helping the scorpion locate prey and navigate its nocturnal world. The ultimate nocturnal navigator, sensing every tremor!

22. Meet the webspinner. Found in tropical regions, it is quite a marvel. This insect doesn't just produce silk; it's the only insect known to produce silk for its entire life. It uses this silk to construct intricate tunnels and chambers, creating a protective fortress. Nature's most dedicated silk weaver and architect combined!

23. Mudskippers, the acrobats of the fish world, are next. Found in the mangrove swamps of Asia and Africa, they use their fins to walk on land, and their slimy skin helps them slide through their muddy homes. When their skin starts to dry out, they use their tongues to wet them, allowing them to stay out of water for hours.

24. Next, slide under the microscope to meet the planarians, flatworms with a knack for regeneration! Cut one into pieces, and watch in awe as each piece transforms into its own complete organism, brain, and all! A microscopic journey of rebirth and transformation!

25. Scuttling across the forest floor, the peanut head bug is a master of illusion. Its head, shaped like a peanut, isn't just a quirky feature—it's a natural defense strategy. This deceptive look confuses predators, who might pass it by, mistaking it for a harmless nut rather than a tasty snack. It's the ultimate camouflage artist, turning a nutty appearance into a survival advantage!

26. Trekking through the thorny terrains of Africa, you almost step on a dried leaf. No, wait! That's the thistle mantis. Resembling a dried thistle or leaf, it's a true master of deception. It's waiting patiently for its next unsuspecting meal to approach. Once prey approaches, the thistle mantis grabs its prey with long arms. A reminder to constantly watch your step!

27. Here come the comb jellies! Found in oceans worldwide, they use hair-like cilia and a gel-like mucus layer to swim smoothly and consume plankton. These hungry hunters eat up to 10 times their weight in one day!

28. Wading in from North America's wetlands, the American bittern is a master of camouflage. This bird's striped plumage looks just like the tall reeds that it inhabits. When threatened, it stretches its neck and points its bill upwards, blending in seamlessly. A bird that reads the reeds to know just how to hide!

29. Ready for a creature that's bound to make your skin crawl? Creeping into the intricate world of spiders, where lost legs are not the end! They can regenerate their complex legs after molting, a process that might take several molts to complete. A web-tastic tale of arachnid recovery!

30. Fluttering from tropical Asia, the dead-leaf butterfly is a marvel of mimicry. When its wings are closed, it resembles a dried leaf with veins. But when it opens its wings, it displays a vibrant pattern of colors. Nature's instinctive 'quick change' artist!

31. Sneaking right in are the Green Lacewing larvae. These tiny tricksters don a cloak of debris to blend seamlessly into their surroundings, and then they sneak up on aphids like ninjas at night. And with one quick jab from their sharp mouth, they enjoy a juicy aphid snack. A gardener's best friend!

32. Taking a deep dive, we encounter the diving bell spider. This spider is the only one of its kind to live entirely underwater. It creates a bubble of air around its abdomen, which allows it to breathe underwater, much like its own personal diving bell. The aquatic world's most unique arachnid!

33. Madagascar's eyelash leaf-tailed gecko is a master of disguise. This gecko's body and tail have irregular edges and patterns, making it look just like a dead leaf, helping it hide from predators. A resourceful lizard with a knack for using fall foliage to its advantage!

34. Salamanders have a slick trick for staying moist: a layer of slippery, slimy mucus. This icky coating makes it hard for predators to grab the salamander. Some even add toxins to the mix, turning themselves into quite the unappetizing meal.

35. Jetting over to the rainforests of Brazil, the Brazilian treehopper sports a helmet that's really the talk of the canopy. But this helmet isn't just a jungle fashion statement; it's studded with symbiotic bacteria, helping to ward off predators like birds and more giant insects. Brazil's top headgear trendsetter!

36. Get out your microscopes- here come the slime molds. Found in forests and on decaying logs, these gooey packs of microorganisms may look like fungi, but they are a unique group of protists. These single-celled organisms can even navigate mazes to find food - quite the microscopic marvel!

37. Dive deep into the Pacific Ocean, where the sea cucumbers make their home. With their simple, elongated shapes and often vibrant colors, they have a certain charm. But don't be fooled! When threatened, they showcase a grotesque defense mechanism - spewing their internal organs out in a sticky mess. Yet, fear not! They regenerate these organs in just a few weeks. Quite the resilient bunch!

38. Meet the velvet worms; from the prehistoric jungles to today's tropical forests, these critters have a unique way of catching dinner. They squirt strands of sticky slime at their prey. Once hit, the slime hardens, ensuring their meal can't wriggle away. Talk about a timeless dinner strategy!

39. Swinging our attention to the dense rainforests of Central Africa, meet the okapi! This relative of the giraffe comes equipped with an 18-inch tongue for buffet-like leaf plucking, self-grooming, and even ear and eye cleaning. The tongue is covered with thick, gooey saliva, which allows the okapi to feast on crunchy sticks and plants. Now that's a practical multi-tool!

40. Deep in the shadows, the assassin bug is on the hunt. Not only is it a silent killer, but it also proudly wears the exoskeletons of its prey as armor. Once it immobilizes its prey, it injects enzymes that liquefy their insides. It's the ultimate insect vampire with a flair for fashion!

41. Look, adventurers, the hardy tardigrades are changing before our eyes! Found everywhere, from the deep sea to the highest mountains, they can survive extreme conditions by producing a protective slime layer. Dehydrate them, and they curl into a dormant form known as a tun. Add water, and voila, they spring back to life!

42. Buzzing into the spotlight is the Katydid. This green insect is often mistaken for a leaf due to its shape and color. With long antennae and powerful hind legs, it's a fascinating critter that sings the songs of summer nights. This bug has a natural way of saying, "Leaf me alone!"

43. All aboard, intrepid explorers! Onward to the dense forests of Madagascar. Amidst the towering trees and echoing calls of lemurs, the giraffe weevil stretches its elongated neck up to three times the length of its body. This isn't just for show; it's a tool for intense male duels and crafting the perfect leafy nest. Oh, and those high-reaching leaves? An easy peasy snack for this long-necked wonder. Madagascar's own neck-and-neck champion!

44. Now, let's meet the caddisfly larva, nature's little architect. This larva is found in freshwater habitats and builds a protective case from materials like stones, sand, or plant material. This case provides shelter and acts as camouflage, showcasing the larva's ingenuity. A tiny but mighty little hider!

45. Squeak squeak! Hear that? Time to explore the fascinating world of mice and their extraordinary livers! Like humans, they can regenerate their liver tissue after injury or partial removal. An enormous feat for such a tiny critter!

46. Let's plunge into the deep with lobsters, another regenerating marvel of the sea! They can regrow their claws, legs, antennae, and entire limbs, bouncing back from battles and encounters with predators. A claw-dropping story of resilience!

47. Flexing its muscles in Central and South America, the Hercules beetle showcases nature's raw power. It is one of the most giant beetles in the world and can carry up to 850 times its body weight. The true heavyweight champion of the beetle world!

48. Fluttering through the night sky, the peppered moth is a living lesson in adaptability. Found in Britain, its coloration changed during the Industrial Revolution. The darker form became more common in polluted areas, while the lighter form thrived in cleaner regions. A unique bug keen to adapt by any means necessary!

49. In the enchanting nooks of the forest, the scorpionfly male is quite romantic. His scorpion-like tail isn't just for looks; it's his secret to winning hearts. He uses it to carry and offer tasty treats, like delicious morsels, to impress the female scorpionflies. It's like a fairy tale in the insect world, where charming gestures and delightful gifts spell love in the air!

50. The mata mata turtles, masters of disguise, are next. Found in the slow-moving freshwater streams and pools of the Amazon and Orinoco basins in South America, they have flat, slimy heads covered in skin flaps. This camouflages them amidst leaf litter, making them nearly invisible to their next meal – fish. Watch out, fish!

51. Crawl over and meet our next camouflage expert, the cryptic mantis. Hailing from Africa, this insect is a marvel in mimicry. Its body, adorned with lobes and intricate patterns, looks like dead leaves and twigs. A cryptic creature hiding in plain sight!

52. Hiding away in Africa, the ghost mantis is a leafy wonder! This crafty bug has a delicate body that mimics the curves and textures of dried leaves, making it a master of disguise in its environment. I be-leaf this critter is as camouflaged as they come!

53. Let's sneak through the arid landscapes of Africa with the spiny mouse! This unique mammal can regrow skin, hair follicles, sweat glands, and even cartilage after an injury. It's a spiky adventure of escape and renewal in the wild!

54. Our next sea critter has eight extraordinary ways that they can reinvent themselves! That's right! Octopuses are the true masters of arm regeneration! Lose an arm to a predator? They can regrow it, regaining full functionality and dexterity. An arm-azing swirl of recovery and adaptation in the underwater realm!

55. Meet the decorator crab, the ocean's do-it-yourself expert. This crab picks up bits of algae, sponges, and other materials from its environment and attaches them to its shell, creating a personalized camouflage. From drab to crab!

56. As dawn breaks in Asia, the spiny flower mantis dazzles us with its vibrant colors. But it unfurls its wings when danger approaches, revealing two large eyespots. These eyespots are designed to resemble larger animals' eyes, helping scare off potential predators. The ultimate showstopper of the insect world!

57. Ahoy! Let's set sail to meet the octopus, the master of masquerade. Specifically, species like the common octopus and mimic octopus are known for their camouflage abilities. With a flick and a twist, they can change their color, texture, and even shape, all thanks to some nifty cells called chromatophores. One moment, it's there, and the next, poof! It's vanished!

58. Eek, here come the eels! Found in both saltwater and freshwater habitats worldwide, these slimy, slithery globetrotters start life as transparent, slimy larvae drifting with ocean currents. After moving to freshwater, they begin to develop, becoming the elongated creatures we know.

59. Flying into the heart of Central and South America, the great potoo takes a daytime siesta. This bird is so well-camouflaged with its bark-like feathers that you might mistake it for a tree branch. It's nature's way of playing hide and seek!

60. All aboard to our next destination— Southeast Asia, home of the sticky frogs. The sticky frogs have adhesive toes, letting them cling to nearly any surface. Their toes are covered in slimy, sticky goo that helps them hold onto trees, walls, and even glass — nothing's too slick for these climbers!

61. Meet a stellar fish with the power to remake itself, the starfish! A real star of the sea, these creatures are regeneration wizards, able to regrow lost limbs and, in some cases, transform a severed limb into an entirely new starfish. The real star of regeneration!

62. Speaking of sea creatures, here come the sea hares. When threatened, they eject a cloud of purple stinky ink, which sends predators running. The ink contains a sticky chemical called opaline, which gets inside the noses of other animals and confuses them. Think of it as a smelly invisibility cloak!

63. Next, let's turn to the banana slugs. These gastropods from the Pacific Northwest are bona fide slime chefs! They whip up slime to lubricate their trails, moisturize their skin, and scare away predators. And talk about recycling — they even consume their own slime to reuse its nutrients! Quite the eco-friendly fellows, wouldn't you say?

64. Dive into the ocean depths to meet the flounder, a flatfish with a flair for fashion. It has a unique ability that allows it to adjust its coloration to match the ocean floor. With both eyes on one side of its body, it can watch predators and prey alike.

65. As we fly into North America, the wheel bug is ready to impress us. But that cogwheel-like structure on its back called the "pronotum," isn't just for show. It serves as armor, protecting the wheel bug from predators and playing a role in thermoregulation. North America's gearhead of the insect realm with a functional flair!

66. Fluttering over to the vibrant meadows of Southeast Asia, we're drawn to a beautiful flower. Oh, wait! It's actually the orchid mantis in disguise. With its petal-like legs, this master of deception can change its hue to match its floral surroundings, luring in pollinators with its blooming allure. Nature's very own chameleon of the bug world!

67. Let's journey to the freshwater habitats of Africa, where the African lungfish thrive. During droughts, these ingenious creatures whip up a mucus sleeping bag and hibernate, waiting for the sweet sound of rainfall. They can bide their time for months, even years. Patience is truly a virtue!

68. From snowy surprise to rocky imitator, the Arctic fox, hailing from the chilly Arctic regions, has a wardrobe that would make any fashionista jealous! In winter, its thick white coat blends in with the snow, while in summer, it sports a brown or gray coat to match the tundra's rocky terrain. Another of nature's witty wardrobe changes!

69. Next, let's leap into the world of geckos, where losing a tail is no big deal! They can break off their tails to escape predators and then later regrow them, balancing and moving as if nothing happened. It's quite the tale of survival and regeneration in the reptile world!

70. Slide over to the giant African land snails, creatures that leave a trail of detection. They emit a slime trail with their unique 'scent,' helping their fellow snails find them. With shells growing up to 8 inches long, these supersized slimy snails are hard to miss!

71. Swim with the zebrafish, the little fish with a big heart—literally! They can regrow their own heart tissue after an injury, a fascinating ability that scientists are studying to unlock secrets for humans. A heartwarming tale of healing and hope under the sea!

72. Now, let's meet the see-through glass frogs. Found in the rainforests of Central and South America, their clear, slippery skin is so translucent that you can see their hearts beating underneath. The lack of color in their skin helps them blend into their leafy environments. A bit unnerving but absolutely fascinating.

73. Ribbit ribbit! Do you hear that? Nestled in the damp forests of Vietnam, the mossy frog is a natural illusionist. Its bumpy, irregular skin, painted in a green, brown, and white mosaic, allows it to vanish against the backdrop of moss-covered rocks and lichens. This frog's remarkable camouflage makes it nearly invisible in its habitat, a true master of blending in with the rocky, verdant landscape. Nature's camouflage rockstar!

74. Let's muck through the mud to meet the geoduck clams of the Pacific Northwest. Their long, rubbery, snorkel-like siphon allows them to dig deep for its food. The siphon works like a straw, sucking up water and tiny food particles. Their odd hunting habits help them live up to their name— "geoduck" comes from the Native American word "gweduc," meaning "dig deep."

75. Crayfish are here to claw their way into your heart! Lose a limb? No problem! These creatures can regrow lost claws or legs, returning to their fully functional selves. It's a magical claw-back story in the freshwater world!

76. Get ready to be inspired by the resilient fiddler crab! Lose a claw? It's just a temporary setback! They can regenerate lost claws over a series of molts, returning to their whole, functional selves. It's a claw-some tale of recovery and renewal on the sandy shores!

77. Hop over to North America to meet the snowshoe hare, nature's trendsetter. This hare changes its coat color in response to the seasons, ensuring it remains camouflaged against predators. Sporting a brown coat in summer and a snowy white one in winter, it's always dressed for the occasion!

78. Dig out those snorkels, and let's dive into the colorful and resilient world of coral! When damaged, they don't just give up. Instead, they regenerate, repair, and regrow their skeleton and tissue, creating a thriving underwater paradise for countless marine species! A colorful dance of survival.

SAGA OF SYMBIOSIS & SURVIVAL

79. Say hi to the Hairworm, nature's escape artist! This noodle-shaped parasite sneaks into crickets and grasshoppers to feast on the fat of these bugs! But the real twist: When the Hairworm is fully mature, it plays puppet master with the insects' minds, making them want to take a swim. The worm exits as the bug takes the dive, swimming to freedom. Talk about a dramatic exit!

80. In the lush rainforests of Central and South America, the conga ant makes its presence known. This impressive ant, recognized for its significant size and strong mandibles, is infamous for its sting, which delivers a sensation like an intense, sharp jab. The conga ant is a small but mighty creature, commanding respect for its potent sting despite its diminutive stature. It's a remarkable example of nature's ability to pack a powerful punch in tiny packages!

81. We're rolling into the grasslands of South America to meet the Armadillo. This armored warrior has a secret trick. When danger lurks, it curls into a nearly impenetrable ball, shielded on all sides. It's digging intricate burrows with powerful legs when it's not playing hide-and-seek. A true architect of the animal kingdom!

82. Enter the Sundew Plant, the sticky star of our show! With its leaves dripping in glistening and sticky goo, it lures bugs into a treacherous tango. As they dance and dart, trying to escape, the plant slowly wraps them up in sticky goo, keeping them for a later feast. Nature's very own sticky trap!

83. These birds want you to save the drama for another mama! The cuckoo bird sneaks her eggs into other birds' nests, tricking them into babysitting! And here's the really cuckoo part: the cuckoo chick is like the big, bossy sibling, hatching first and sometimes kicking out the other eggs or chicks. Quite the attention hogger, isn't it?

84. Slinking from tree to tree, our next creature is a sight! In the rainforests of Africa, the African bush viper dazzles us with its bright colors. But don't be fooled by its vivid rainbow of scales; its venom can cause severe harm. A beauty with a bite!

85. Now, let's traverse the arid deserts of the Middle East, but watch your step! The venomous deathstalker scorpion scuttles beneath our feet, ready to defend against predators. This sneaky little arachnid may be crawling through laboratories, too, as it's being eyed for potential medical marvels!

86. Down deep into the ocean's embrace, the Pygmy Whale awaits. It has a unique defense. When threatened, the pygmy whale releases a cloud of dark ink, then vanishes, leaving predators baffled. A true master of the oceanic vanishing act!

87. Catch a wave over to the Caribbean, where we find the "tree of death," the manchineel tree. Its fruits resemble small apples, but beware! Its sap can cause blisters, and even its raindrops are a menace. However, its wood is used for making furniture once it's dried and treated. That's a painful price to pay for furnishings!

88. Ever heard of real-life zombies? The zombie-ant fungus is here to spook you! This crafty fungus takes over carpenter ants, making them climb high into the trees and then... BOOM! The fungus sprouts right out of the ant's head, releasing its spores to create more ant zombies. It's a tale straight out of a scary movie!

89. Head down under and say hello to the capybara, nature's own furry ecosystem! These giant, friendly rodents are like a playground for birds, such as the wattled jacana. The birds love to munch on all the tiny critters that live in the capybara's fur. It's great: the capybaras get a bug-free fur coat, and the birds get a tasty snack. It's like having a party on their back!

90. Trudging into the swamps of South America, the lancehead pit viper slithers by. With its triangular head and unique patterns, this snake has venom that can be a handful to its unsuspecting prey. But these snakes are also saving lives; their potent venom is used to make medications to treat high blood pressure!

91. Get low to see our next fearsome-looking creature! Across the forest floors of the Americas, the New World tarantulas crawl. While this creature can be quite alarming in size, you'll find that they are more about the show than the bite. Their venom is mild, but their urticating hairs can cause irritation. A prickly situation, indeed!

92. Is it a vine or a rope? Oh no, it's another snake! Look high towards the trees in the wetlands of Asia. Here, we will discover the boomslang snake dangling from tree branches. With its large eyes, this green and black snake has venom that affects the blood's ability to clot. Just one bite can cause severe internal and external bleeding. A leafy lurker with quite the bite!

93. Dive deep with the Snapping Shrimp and its trusty sidekick, the Goby fish. The shrimp digs a cozy burrow while the fish keeps watch. If danger approaches, the fish gives a warning flick, and both dive safely. In return, the shrimp shares its meals with the Goby fish. Talk about the ultimate underwater friendship!

94. Plunging deeper into the coral reefs of the Indo-Pacific, the cone snails await. With their intricate patterns, these spiral-shelled wonders use their venom to gently catch tiny fish. And guess what? Scientists are studying their venom for clues to make new medicines. It's like they're tiny pharmacists of the sea!

95. Banana split, anyone? But be careful to avoid encountering our next crawling creature! Typically found roaming South America's forest floors, the Brazilian wandering spider searches for prey. This sizable brown spider is venomous and has a quirky habit: it sometimes stows away in banana shipments. Talk about unexpected cargo!

96. Watch out! Shield your eyes! We are wandering into the deserts of Asia, where the spitting cobra showcases its unique talent. This snake can "spit" venom up to 6 feet away! Wearing some slick shades in its territory is always a good idea. This snake is the spitting image of danger!

97. Head to the forests of North America to find the Eastern Box Turtle. When danger approaches, this turtle can completely close its shell, sealing itself inside with a hinged lower shell. This makes it nearly impossible for predators to grasp it, providing a fortress-like defense. A turtle with a built-in bunker!

98. Now, let's fly over to the forests of Asia, where we meet the dark-winged Asian hornet. With its yellow face, this giant hornet has quite the taste for insects. But be careful! Its venom can be a real drag for humans. Always a good idea to give these busy bugs their space!

99. Think you can spot our next creature? Camouflaged among the rocky and muddy seafloors of the Pacific and Indian Oceans, the stonefish is a master of surprise. When threatened, it raises its venomous spines to defend against predators like sharks. If stepped on by humans, a timely treatment makes this misstep just a painful memory for the unlucky swimmer.

100. Let's meet another sneaky snake on our list. In the grasslands of eastern Australia, the eastern brown snake slithers. With its brown scales, this slender snake is a most venomous force to be reckoned with. But here's a twist: it primarily dines on mice and rats. A rodent's worst nightmare!

101. Buzzing into the scene is the Varroa mite, the bee's worst nightmare. These tiny terrors feast on bee blood, weakening our buzzing buddies and opening the door for deadly diseases. They're the ultimate intruder of the bee world, and they sure know how to make an entrance!

102. Beware the next stop on our journey as we venture deep into the ancient forests of Europe, where we uncover belladonna, also known as deadly nightshade. Its beguiling berries might seem tempting, but they're a cocktail of disaster for our nervous system. In the past, it was also the beauty secret to dilated pupils. Beauty with a touch of danger!

103. Now, suit up and come along as we dive back into the tropical waters of Australia. We'll find the box jellyfish floating gracefully in the shallow waters here. With its cube-shaped bell, this translucent creature has tentacles that can really spell trouble if it lands a highly venomous sting. Protective clothing is a must when diving in its domain!

104. A shy and stealthy critter is next on our list! Scurrying through the deserts of India, we might catch a glimpse of the Indian red scorpion. This small, reddish-brown scorpion has a powerful set of pincers and venom that can be lethal. A tiny desert dancer with a disastrous sting!

105. Our exploration continues deep into the tropical rainforests. Here, the strychnine tree's seeds are a potent toxin. If consumed, it can cause muscle contractions and has even been historically used as rat poison. Tread carefully in nature!

106. Swinging our focus from the trees back down to the ground. Living in the forests of Southeast Asia, the blue krait slithers. With its mix of blue and white, this banded snake is more venomous than even the cobra. But a little-known fact: it's also quite shy. A slithering secret keeper!

107. Prepare to be amazed by the Guinea Worm's grand escape plan! After a year of living inside humans and growing up to 3 feet long, the female worm makes her move. She causes an itchy blister, tempting the human to seek relief in water. And then she releases her young, starting her sneaky cycle over again. Makes you rethink taking a nice swim, doesn't it?

108. Shimmering into the spotlight now is the Jewel Wasp, a dazzling diva with a surprising trick up her sleeve. She's on a mission to find the perfect cockroach for an extraordinary task. With a swift and precise sting, she cleverly turns the roach into a dazed wanderer. After stinging, she lays her egg on this unsuspecting host. As the baby wasp grows, it has its own built-in meal, nibbling on the roach from the inside out. A wild tale of nature's cunning strategies!

109. Next, we're off to the African plains to marvel at the Giraffe. While known for its long neck, its powerful kick is its natural defense. A single kick can shatter bones or even kill a predator. Tall, majestic, and not to be messed with! Talk about a pain in the neck!

110. The early bird gets the worm, or so we thought! The worm, in this case, is instead a stealthy snake! In the rocky terrains of Australia, the death adder lies in ambush. With its viper-like head and thick body, this snake uses its worm-like tail to lure prey. A swift, venomous bite follows. But with timely treatment, it's just a sting in the tale!

111. Dive into the chilly North Atlantic, where the Hooded Seal blows up the competition! It can inflate its nose like a giant red balloon. It's not just for show – this nose knows how to scare off predators and impress friends. Talk about a party trick with a purpose!

112. Venture into the rainforests of Central and South America to discover the incredible Hairy Frogfish. This fascinating creature uses its hair-like skin appendages to blend seamlessly into the surrounding seaweed and coral. This camouflage not only helps it ambush prey but also acts as a defense against predators. It's a master of underwater disguise, looking more like a clump of seaweed than a fish!

113. Step carefully as we venture into the African savannah again. The African Crested Porcupine is on guard! When danger approaches, it's all about the rattle and roll. With quills standing tall, it's ready to charge, turning any predator into a pincushion. That's a prickly problem for predators!

114. Swinging through the depths of the Southeast Asian jungles, the Malayan Colugo glides from tree to tree. This nocturnal mammal has a membrane between its limbs that acts like a built-in flight suit, allowing it to glide through the air effortlessly, escaping predators by air. Nature's ultimate skydiver!

115. Do you hear that, animal adventurers? Why, it sounds like a rattlesnake, but wait, that isn't a rattlesnake at all! In the forests of North America, the Eastern Indigo Snake has a unique defense. When threatened, it mimics a rattlesnake's rattle, despite being non-venomous, to scare off predators. What a devious defense!

116. You might want to hug our next adorable animal, but beware! Found climbing trees in the rainforests of Southeast Asia, this creature's bite can deliver a toxic surprise from glands near its elbows. Who is this adorable creature with round eyes and soft fur? It's the slow loris! Who knew a critter so cute could be so cunning?

117. Hiking forward into the sunny heaths and woodlands of the United Kingdom, the peculiarly patterned European adder basks. This zigzag-patterned snake can deliver a mildly venomous bite but mostly keeps to itself. A sun-loving serpent!

118. Plummeting below the surface of the coastal waters of Australia, the blue-ringed octopus dazzles with its vibrant colors. But don't be fooled. It can deliver a very venomous bite when threatened. A bite for which there's no known antivenom. Beauty with a bite!

119. Digging deeper now, here we go! Within the gardens and fields of Europe, the European mole digs. With its spade-like hands, this small, velvety mammal burrows underground in search of insects. Its venomous saliva can paralyze its prey, ensuring a fresh meal. What a subterranean surprise!

120. Snorkels ready? Goggles on? Dive in and come take a look! Deep in the coral reefs of the Caribbean, the fire coral stands. With its branching structures, this unique orange-red marine wonder isn't genuine coral but a hydrozoan. Its sting can cause severe pain, significantly if predators like parrotfish threaten it. A reef's fiery facade!

121. Now, let's zoom into the world of the bedbug, the ultimate hide-and-seek champion. These tiny terrors have a taste for blood, leaving itchy bites as reminders of their visits. And here's the kicker: they can play quite the waiting game, going without a meal for up to a whole year. Talk about patience!

122. Watch out for that bird! Best to avoid our next flighty defender as we soar to the skies to view the Eurasian Capercaillie. At times, the male can become so aggressive that it will attack anything, including predators and humans, making it a formidable opponent despite its size.

123. Buckle up for the tale of the cunning Sacculina barnacle! Picture this: a barnacle larva hijacks a crab. Once inside the crab, it morphs into spooky, root-like threads that steal all the crab's nutrients. But here's where it gets wild - the crab gets so mind-whammied that it thinks the parasite's eggs are its own babies and takes care of them. Quite the crabby conundrum!

124. Next on our list is the Ichneumon Wasp, the ultimate insect infiltrator. She's on a mission, and it's not for nectar but for insect larvae. Once she finds her target, she injects her eggs inside the unsuspecting larvae. As the eggs hatch, the baby wasps make their way out of the larvae by feasting from the inside, ensuring the balance of the insect kingdom remains intact.

125. Let's march with a harmonious tale of the Myrmecophyte plants and ants. Picture this: the plants offer ants a fancy shelter and sweet treats. To say thanks, the ants roll up their sleeves and guard their green guardians from hungry herbivores that dare to try to eat them. It's nature's version of roommates in perfect harmony!

126. In the dense forests of Southeast Asia, meet the Malayan Flying Fox. This giant bat has a unique defense - it can emit a loud, high-pitched sound that disorients predators. Additionally, its ability to fly and roost high in the trees keeps it out of reach from many ground-based threats. An aerial acrobat with a sonic shield!

127. Ouch! Those sharp spines won't allow us to forget the Hedgehog! This piercing critter is a small but mighty creature found in Europe and Asia. When threatened, it rolls into a tight ball, presenting a fortress of spiky quills to any attacker. A prickly ball of defense!

128. Skimming over to the shallow waters of the Great Barrier Reef, the Irukandji jellyfish floats. This tiny, transparent marvel has venom that can cause severe pain. But here's an unusual twist: its sting can also lead to a feeling of unease. A small package with a big punch!

129. Charmingly nestled on the forest floors of Europe, the death cap mushroom stands proudly with its umbrella-like cap. This greenish-brown fungus can cause severe liver damage to those who dare to try. Remember, kids, not all mushrooms are meant for munching!

130. Hold onto your hats because we're not done yet! Our next stop is in Australia to find the Thorny Devil. This spiky lizard has a body covered in hard, sharp spikes, making it a challenging meal to swallow. Plus, it can collect water in the desert by channeling dew and rain to its mouth through its skin. A true desert survivor!

131. Next, a tale of hide-and-leap with the Trapdoor Spider! This sneaky spider sits silently in its secret shelter, with a perfectly camouflaged door. And when a bug strolls by, surprise! Out jumps the spider, securing its supper in a split second. Peekaboo with a predatory twist!

132. The floor will undoubtedly feel like lava if we step on our next intimidating insect! In the rainforests of Central and South America, the little fire ants march. If you don't tread carefully, these tiny reddish ants deliver a sting that feels like a small blaze. A double dose of fire!

133. Our next flower may look like it belongs in an elegant bouquet, but don't be fooled! Wandering through the meadows of North America, we encounter the hemlock plant standing tall. But its delicate white flowers are hiding a secret: poison. Poison hemlock has a notorious spot in the tales of ancient Greece, while water hemlock holds the title for being exceptionally toxic. Nature's duality at its finest!

134. It might be time to buzz over and visit our next creature. The Africanized honey bee buzzes about in the tropical regions of Africa and the Americas. With its golden-brown color, this small bee is a hybrid with a temper. Its venom isn't more potent than regular honeybees, but they attack in more significant numbers. A buzzing brigade of fury!

135. Journey to the dense forests of Southeast Asia to meet the Draco Lizard. This remarkable reptile has extendable wing-like flaps of skin on its sides, which it uses to glide from tree to tree. This ability not only helps it escape predators but also travel across the forest without having to descend to the dangerous forest floor. It's like a miniature dragon taking flight!

136. Next on our journey, we discover a monster that lurks deep in the deserts of the southwestern US and Mexico...a Gila monster, that is! This cleverly named creature is, in fact, a venomous lizard. It might have a fearsome name, but it's more about the show than the bite. And here's a less-than-monstrous twist: its venom has paved the way for a type of diabetes medication!

137. Time to spread our wings and flutter into the moonlit nights of Europe. This is where you'll find the death's-head hawkmoth. This giant moth, with its skull-like pattern and yellow and black body, is a nocturnal navigator. It's known to raid beehives for honey, and its eerie squeak can be quite unsettling. A winged whisperer of the night!

138. Step right up and witness the antlion's sandy spectacle! This crafty critter carves out a pit where it waits patiently for a bug to blunder inside. And when they do? A flurry of sand sends them spiraling right into the antlion's waiting jaws. It's like a desert whirlwind with a twist!

139. Watch your step as we traverse the dense rainforests of Central and South America, where we stumble upon the poison dart frog. Don't be fooled by its vibrant colors; this tiny amphibian's skin carries enough toxin to deter any would-be predator. Indigenous tribes even use its venom for their blow darts!

140. Shh! Do you hear that rattling sound? In the arid regions of the Americas, the rattlesnake coils. The rattle at the end of its tail serves as a warning to anyone who comes too close. Beware; its venom can be incredibly potent, so listen closely for its warning before you come near! This snake is a regular hissing herald of the Wild West indeed!

141. Creeping and crawling around North America's basements and dark corners, the black widow spider weaves its intricate web. With its iconic red hourglass marking, this shiny black spider has venom that can be quite a handful! But here's a twist: the females sometimes dine on their mates. A tragic love story!

142. Swimming right along the freshwater streams of eastern Australia, the quirky platypus swims. This egg-laying mammal has a secret weapon: the males sport venomous spurs on their hind legs that can deliver a painful sting. Nature's adorable oddball holds a prickly surprise!

143. Next, let's meet the Lancet Liver Fluke, the ultimate mastermind of the parasitic world! Its master plan: to inhabit the insides of a large grazing animal, such as a cow or sheep! However, it starts out small, living inside a snail, then hops onto an ant when it's ready for its grand plan to hatch. Finally, it plays a little mind control game, making the ant climb grass blades! Voila, now it's a prime snack for its target: grazing animals! A round of applause for this sneaky strategist!

144. Shhh! Try not to startle our next slithering subject. Quickly and quietly through the arid regions of Australia, the elusive inland taipan snake slithers. Growing up to 8 feet, its venom is no joke. One bite can spell doom for multiple humans. But fear not; this reclusive reptile mostly keeps to itself!

145. Splash! A unique creature awaits us within the warm waters of the Atlantic! The unusual Portuguese man o' war floats in wait. With its blue and purple hues, this marine marvel isn't a jellyfish but a siphonophore. Its tentacles can deliver an excruciating sting indeed. A floating fortress of fury!

146. Now, imagine a pitcher. It's not filled with lemonade this time, but it is instead a sticky trap! The Pitcher Plant draws bugs into its sticky pitchers with a sugary scent they can't resist. But woe to those who venture in, for they'll find themselves sliding down to a sticky end. A pitcher-perfect trap, if you ask me!

147. How about a bug-sized horror story? Meet the Xenos vesparum, the puppet master of the insect world. This sneaky bug takes over young wasps, turning them into its personal drones. It tricks the wasps into carrying its eggs to the perfect spot. When the eggs hatch, the cycle starts all over again with new wasps. It's a never-ending parasite parade!

148. Gardeners beware! In Mediterranean gardens, we are bound to meet the oleander, an ornamental shrub with beautiful pink or white flowers. Be aware of its beauty, though. This shrub is a known master of disguise whose extracts also served as ancient arrow poisons. Beauty that's more than skin deep!

149. Slithering back to the grasslands of Africa, the puff adder lies in wait. This thick-bodied snake, with its unique patterns, has a venomous reputation. Its bite can cause severe tissue damage. But here's a quirky fact: it's also one of the fastest-striking snakes. Talk about grabbing a quick bite!

150. Our next defense is sure to leave a mark! In the Arctic tundra, the Musk Ox forms a defensive circle with its young in the center, presenting a wall of horns to approaching predators, a testament to the power of unity in defense.

151. In the darkness lurks a creature that sends shivers down the bravest spines: the vampire bat. This nocturnal dweller prowls the night, seeking something most peculiar: the taste of blood to feed a diet known as hematophagy. But don't fret; it approaches its prey delicately, leaving hardly a trace it was ever feasting on their blood. A nightmarish name for a bat that is undoubtedly no nightmare.

152. Creeping through the Amazon rainforest, the Brazilian Wandering Spider creeps ferociously. When threatened, it raises its body and legs, showing off its enormous fangs, ready to take on predators or threats. A creepy crawler, for sure!

153. Our next slithering friend is as fashionable as they come. Sliding across the dense forests of India and Southeast Asia, we encounter the king cobra. With its flared hood, this majestic snake has a venom that can challenge even an elephant. But here's a fun tidbit: it dines on other snakes. A royal palate, indeed!

154. Deep in the forests of North America, the coral snake slithers. This slender snake, with its vibrant red, yellow, and black bands, is a sight to behold. Its venom can significantly affect the nervous system of those it bites. Nature's rainbow surprise!

155. Ahead, we'll stroll into the suburban areas of New South Wales, where the Sydney funnel-web spider might surprise you. This giant, dark-colored spider is a nightmare for primates and humans due to its highly venomous bite. So step carefully!

156. Now, let's bask in the sun with the Spiny-tailed Iguana. But don't get too close! This seemingly lazy reptile has a tail that's a weapon in disguise. With sharp, pointed scales, it delivers whip-like strikes that make any predator think twice. A tail reminiscent of a dinosaur defense!

157. Grab your safari gear as we visit the savannas of Africa. Here, the acacia ants have struck a deal with the acacia tree. They sip on the tree's nectar and, in return, fiercely guard it against herbivores. They're not just venomous warriors; they're also tree guardians. Nature's security system in action!

158. Sun hats on as we explore the brutal Australian outback. This is where we'll find the Echidna, a spiny anteater! Its best defense is that it can dig itself into the ground, exposing only its sharp spines. A living fortress against any curious predator. Talk about resourcefulness!

159. Back on land, we discover a spider with a violin. But this reclusive arachnid doesn't play beautiful music. In fact, its violin-shaped markings are a warning sign that we've encountered a brown recluse spider. These spiders prefer to stay out of the limelight, hiding in the attics and sheds of North America. Its corrosive venom can leave quite a mark, causing skin lesions. A reminder that sometimes, it's best to let sleeping spiders lie!

160. It's time to shoot for the stars! But not the ones in outer space! Instead, the star of this show lives in the coral reefs of the Pacific. The crown-of-thorns starfish is a spiky marine wonder with multiple arms and sharp spines. They feast on coral polyps and possess venomous spines that remind you to keep your distance. Thank your lucky stars you didn't step on one!

161. Swinging into the plant realm, we meet the Dodder Plant, known as the Witch's Hair. This plant doesn't believe in hard work. Instead, it wraps around other plants, sucking away their nutrients like a botanical bandit. Plants have their own tales of treachery, and this one's a classic!

162. Zap! We're diving deep into the Amazon River, where the Electric Eel lights up the waters. This electrifying creature can send out pulses intense enough to stun its prey. It's like the lightning bolt of the animal world, ensuring the eel always has a charged meal. Electrifying!

163. Next, brace yourselves for the Tongue-Eating Louse, the ultimate identity thief. This tiny terror cozies up to a fish's tongue, sips away until there's nothing left, and then takes the tongue's place! It lives as a pseudo-tongue, dining on the fish's blood and mucus. Talk about a fishy facelift!

164. Look up, adventurers! Growing in tropical regions, the castor bean plant stands tall. While it's well known for giving us castor oil, you might not know that its seeds also harbor ricin, a toxin so potent that even a pinch can wreak havoc on animals and humans alike. But every gift can harbor a secret!

165. Wandering solo through the African grasslands, the reclusive Honey Badger is known for its toughness. This weasel has skin so rigid and loose that it can twist around in its skin to bite back when grabbed by a predator. A story of animal defense with a literal twist!

166. Next, we must pull on our gloves to explore the rainforests of northern Australia! Because here we encounter the gympie-gympie plant. It stands, appearing harmless, with its lovely heart-shaped leaves. But don't be fooled; a mere touch can cause days of discomfort. Ouch!

167. Don your scuba gear, and let's splash into the coastal waters of Japan! Here, we meet the pufferfish. This inflatable wonder, growing up to 35 inches when threatened, carries tetrodotoxin, a toxin that is 1,200 times more poisonous than cyanide! Yet, in Japan, it's a delicacy food prepared by specially trained chefs. Talk about dining on the edge!

168. Up ahead, in the grasslands of Asia, the Russell's viper slithers. With its chain-like patterns, this snake has a venomous bite that can cause severe pain and bleeding. But here's an astonishing fact: its venom is used in several critical diagnostic tests for blood clotting disorders, such as lupus anticoagulant. A slithering superhero!

JOURNEYS & GIANTS: MIGRATION & MEGAFAUNA

169. First up, the monarch butterfly flutters by! Come along on a unique adventure as we fly with these mighty travelers, covering a 3,000-mile journey from North America to Mexico. Remarkably, this migration spans four generations, each playing a role in this incredible relay race against winter. Proof that determination can come in the smallest of packages!

170. Glide through the Ordovician seas with the Cameroceras, an enormous cephalopod. Dominating the ancient oceans about 470 million years ago, its extinction is a story of the ever-changing seas. A shell of a tale from the ocean's depths!

171. Next, Let's embark on a shell-abration of epic proportion as we plunge into the world of green sea turtles! They travel up to 1,400 miles from feeding areas to nesting beaches, often returning to the very beach where they were born. This remarkable homing instinct ensures the continuation of their lineage. The armored navigator of the sea!

172. Peer into Pleistocene Australia at the Diprotodon, the largest known marsupial. Resembling a giant wombat, this gentle herbivore's extinction about 50,000 years ago marks the end of an era for giant marsupials. A wombat-like wave goodbye to a megafauna marvel!

173. Grab your fishing gear, anglers, and meet the Baryonyx! Also known as the ultimate fisherman of the Jurassic, this curious creature had a face like a crocodile and claws that could've been the envy of any seafood chef of the time!

174. Let's giggle at the Gasosaurus, named not for any prehistoric flatulence but for the energy company that stumbled upon its bones. An ironic name that makes everyone who hears it wonder about its gassy past.

175. Step into the Pleistocene to meet the Short-faced Bear. Towering over modern bears, this North American predator's extinction about 11,000 years ago is a story of survival and competition. A bear-sized goodbye to a Pleistocene powerhouse!

176. Behold the tale of Madagascar's extinct elephant bird, the champion of giant eggs! These birds took the crown for the largest egg ever laid by a living creature. They laid eggs up to 34 cm long and 30 cm wide! That's about the size of a basketball! Imagine the omelet you could make with that!

177. Power your brain on with the Troodon! This brainy beast was likely the genius of all dinosaurs! With a noggin that was large for its body size, this smarty-pants dino shows that big brains always have a place, even among the giants!

178. Trek through pre-human New Zealand to find the Moa, towering flightless birds up to 12 feet tall. With no natural predators, they were hunted to extinction by humans by the 1400s. A towering tale of loss in the bird world!

179. You'd better get some rest before this journey, explorers! The journey of the blackpoll warbler is a doozy! These birds fly non-stop for up to 88 hours across the open ocean, covering around 1,700 miles from North America to South America. This incredible feat is one of the longest migrations of any songbird. They say time flies when you're having fun, but for these birds, it's all about finding the perfect vacation spot under the sun!

180. Time to tiptoe around the Argentinosaurus, the hulk of the ancient world. Weighing in at a staggering 100 tons, this gentle giant could make the earth tremble like a living earthquake. Imagine a creature so immense it could wear a necklace of 15 African elephants and still have room for a bow tie!

181. Sneak into the Tasmanian wilderness to glimpse the Tasmanian Tiger. This marsupial with a canine-like appearance and distinct stripes was last seen in 1936. Overhunting, disease, and habitat loss led to its sad extinction. A ghostly goodbye to a striped wonder!

182. Discover something new with the Patagotitan! This giant dino was a recent discovery that just might challenge the Argentinosaurus for the heavyweight title of the dinosaur world. This new kid on the block shows us that there's always something bigger to discover!

183. Buckle up those life vests because we're about to embark on an incredible journey alongside the Pacific salmon! Our brave salmon friends start their epic adventure by diving into the exhilarating river rapids. Swimming against solid currents, these resilient fish make an extraordinary upstream journey to their birthplaces to have their babies in the waters they were born in!. Facing predators and overcoming obstacles, they travel hundreds of miles, showing us that we can conquer any challenge with determination and resilience!

184. Feel that shaking? Here comes the earth-quaking sound of the great wildebeest migration! This awe-inspiring movement across the Serengeti and Maasai Mara involves over a million wildebeest, zebras, and gazelles. They follow the rains in a relentless search for fresh pastures, a journey fraught with peril and triumph. Nature's earth-shattering quest for survival!

185. Let's take a look at the monstrous claws of the Therizinosaurus, but don't fear, they weren't predators! This dino had longer claws than your arm, yet he was the gentle giant of the leafy world. This peaceful plant-eater used its mega claws to reach for the tastiest leaves despite looking like it could star in a dino horror movie.

186. Trek through Madagascar's jungles to meet the Elephant Bird. Weighing up to 1,100 pounds and standing 10 feet tall, this massive bird's extinction in the 17th century is a tale of human impact. A giant eggshell of a story, now just in the past!

187. Are you ready to go on a whale of an adventure? Trace the gray whales' path, the ocean's great migrators. Their round-trip of 12,000 miles from the Arctic to Baja, California, is one of the longest migrations of any mammal. They travel to feed in the nutrient-rich Arctic and breed in the warmer southern waters. A trip that proves these whales are whale-seasoned explorers who certainly know how to make a splash!

188. Time to play a game, adventurers. Can you spot our next dino? The Psittacosaurus was thought to have been the hide-and-seek champion of its time. With a sneaky pattern that blended into the forests, this dino could have given the fiercest predators a real challenge in spotting it. It's the master of dinosaur camouflage!

189. Sneak into Pleistocene Eurasia's forests to spot the Cave Bear. More significant than modern brown bears and revered in ancient art, they vanished about 24,000 years ago, a bear-sized chapter in prehistory closing.

190. Can you imagine a giant, ferocious dino with a fluff of feathers? It might seem a little silly, but this was the life of the Yutyrannus. This dinosaur was a feathery cousin of the T-Rex, which suggests that even the most fearsome dinosaurs might have had a softer side. A truly fashionable predator with a fluffy feather coat!

191. Stay far, far away from the Utahraptor! They may have only been as tall as a human, but these fickle foes had toe claws, a real-life slashing sensation. This dino could have inspired a monster movie, which proves that sometimes, the scariest things come in small (but incredibly sharp) packages!

192. Dance with the plankton as they shimmy up to the surface before nightfall! These tiny organisms undergo a daily vertical migration, rising to the surface at night to feed and sinking during the day to avoid predators. This movement is crucial for the ocean's nutrient cycles and food webs. These little critters show us that you must ebb and flow to stay afloat!

193. Flap alongside the Haast's Eagles, the largest known eagles with a 10-foot wingspan. Native to New Zealand and reliant on the Moa, they vanished around the same time as their prey in the 1400s. An eagle's end is linked to its food chain!

194. Venture into ancient Australia with the Megalania, a giant monitor lizard. This 23-foot-long predator's story, ending about 50,000 years ago, is a tale of a time when giant reptiles roamed the land. A lizard's legacy is now just a fossil tale!

195. Marvel at the Kosmoceratops, with a crown of horns and hooks, it was the true royal of the dinosaur kingdom. This dino's headgear was so fancy it could have walked the red carpet of the Cretaceous period and stolen the show!

196. Let's flap our wings in the night with the straw-colored fruit bats. About 10 million bats converge yearly in Zambia's Kasanka National Park. They migrate to feast on the abundant fruit, creating the world's most giant mammal migration spectacle. A bat with a migration based on the needs of its belly!

197. Delve into ancient seas with the Trilobite, a diverse group of marine arthropods that thrived for over 270 million years. These ancient ocean dwellers, ranging from tiny to over a foot long, were the rulers of the Cambrian seas. A long reign, now just a fossil memory!

198. Shark cages deployed; now it's time for us to swim with the hammerhead sharks on their mysterious ocean journey. These sharks gather in large schools and migrate for reasons not fully understood, possibly for feeding or breeding. They navigate vast distances, following the ocean's invisible pathways. A shark that goes with the flow, bringing along a few friends!

199. Plunge into the Cambrian seas to meet the Anomalocaris, a peculiar prehistoric predator. With its large eyes and circular mouth, this 3-foot-long creature vanished over 500 million years ago. A curious chapter in the ocean's prehistoric tale!

200. Amble with the Giant Ground Sloth in South America. These enormous herbivores, some as big as elephants, disappeared around 10,000 years ago, likely due to climate change and hunting. A slow stroll into history for these gentle giants!

201. Dive with me into the ancient oceans to spot the Megalodon, a massive shark that could reach 60 feet in length. Ruling as a top predator, its decline around 2.6 million years ago was likely due to changing climates and dwindling prey. A titanic tale of the deep!

202. Gaze up at the skies of 19th-century North America, once teeming with Passenger Pigeons. Known for their massive flocks, they were hunted to extinction, with the last one dying in 1914. A final flight for the feathered multitudes!

203. Stomp over to the Eocene era with the Andrewsarchus, known for its massive skull. Possibly one of the largest terrestrial carnivorous mammals, it's a story of a mighty predator now lost to time. A jaw-dropping end to a prehistoric giant!

204. Listen for the echo of the Parasaurolophus, the Mesozoic's natural musician. Its unique crest, resembling a built-in trumpet, might have allowed this dinosaur to produce otherworldly sounds, serenading the ancient forests with a melody as striking as its appearance.

205. Be amazed by the Deinocheirus, a dinosaur that's full of surprises! Initially identified by its enormous arms, this creature was later revealed to be a humpbacked marvel with an appetite for fish. Sporting a duck-like bill and a camel-like body, the Deinocheirus was a unique blend of features, showcasing some of nature's most unusual and fantastic designs in one extraordinary dinosaur.

206. Are you ready to adventure across the Pacific with the leatherback sea turtles? These ancient mariners travel over 6,000 miles from their feeding grounds in the jellyfish-rich waters to the nesting beaches. They undertake this vast journey to lay eggs, ensuring the survival of their species. A species dedicated to living out their ancient legacy.

207. Wander through the southeastern U.S. forests, once home to the Carolina Parakeet. North America's only native parrot, known for its vibrant colors, was lost to habitat destruction and hunting by the early 20th century. A colorful curtain call for a vibrant bird!

208. Dancing into the spotlight, meet Sinosauropteryx, the feathered star of the dinosaur era. This little predator rocked a fabulous feather coat, dazzling enough to make any bird pause and admire and turn our old ideas of dinosaurs on their head!

209. Hold onto your hooves, adventurers, as we track the epic trek of the caribou across the Arctic tundra. Covering up to 3,000 miles annually, they migrate in large herds, facing predators and harsh conditions. This journey is one of the most prolonged and arduous of any terrestrial mammal. A caribou-tiful display of epic determination!

210. Can you imagine a beach entirely covered in crabs? March on over and witness the red crabs of Christmas Island. Millions of crabs journey from the forest to the coast each year to breed and release eggs. This synchronized migration transforms the island into a spectacular display of nature's timing and precision. Indeed, it is a startling and scuttling sight to see!

211. Marvel at the Irish Elk in ancient forests and grasslands. Renowned for its massive 12-foot antlers and standing 7 feet at the shoulder, it roamed Europe and Asia before vanishing around 7,700 years ago. A majestic end to an antlered king!

212. Stomping in with a roar is one earthshaking dinosaur. Make way for the mighty Tyrannosaurus rex! The T-Rex is the undisputed king of lizards with a jaw strength of up to 3000 pounds per square inch. However, we should call them the undisputed queens since the female T-Rex was the largest of these species! With a roar that echoes through time, this dino is a timeless icon of the prehistoric world!

213. Could you imagine a dinosaur so long that it could stretch the length of an entire basketball court? The Supersaurus certainly lives up to its super name, as it's believed to have been the longest dinosaur ever!

214. Up, up into the sky with the Arctic tern, the ultimate long-distance flyer! These birds make an astonishing journey from their Arctic breeding grounds to the Antarctic and back each year, covering about 25,000 miles. With this wild journey, it's no wonder they see more daylight than any other creature on earth.

215. Ready for a long trip? Fly far, everyone, and we'll circle the continents with the white stork. These birds travel up to 6,200 miles between their European breeding grounds and African wintering grounds. They rely on thermal updrafts to glide long distances, conserving energy on their intercontinental voyage. These feathered voyagers are always in search of the sunshine!

216. Boing-Boing! Time to bound through the Australian outback with the red kangaroo. These marsupials don't migrate long distances but move opportunistically in response to rainfall and food availability, covering large areas in their search for sustenance. A creature bouncing across the land to find everything it needs to survive!

217. Look back to the Permian period at the Dimetrodon, a predator with a distinctive sail. This mammal precursor, roaming about 295 million years ago, used its sail for body temperature regulation. A sail into extinction for a prehistoric icon!

218. Roll with the Glyptodon, an armadillo-like creature with a protective shell. Roaming the Americas during the Pleistocene, this herbivore's extinction around 10,000 years ago marks the end of an armored era. A shell-shocked goodbye to a unique herbivore!

219. Navigate South America's ancient rivers to spot the Purussaurus, a gigantic caiman. This 41-foot-long apex predator's story from 8 million years ago is a reminder of the prehistoric giants that once ruled the waters. A titanic tale of a river ruler!

220. Remember to eat your vegetables with the Nothronychus! This dino shows us that change is always possible. Starting life as a meat-eater and switching to plants, this dino reminds you that you can always turn over a new leaf.

221. Time for a name mix-up! The dinosaur named Oviraptor, which means "egg snatcher," was once thought to steal other dinosaurs' eggs. But newer discoveries suggest a different story. It turns out the Oviraptor might have been a caring parent, not a thief. Evidence shows them fossilized over their own nests, protectively embracing their eggs, hinting at a nurturing side rather than the egg-stealing behavior initially assumed.

222. Soar over the Cretaceous skies with me to see the Quetzalcoatlus. With a wingspan of 36 feet, it was one of the largest flying animals ever. Its extinction, part of a massive event that ended the Cretaceous period, marked the fall of a sky giant!

223. Brace yourself for a fantastic adventure as we dive into the currents of the sardine run. This massive migration of sardines along South Africa's coast creates a feeding frenzy for predators. The run occurs when billions of sardines spawn in the cool waters and then move northward. A spectacular sardine run, indeed!

224. Get ready to spread your wings and join the painted parade as these beautiful butterflies flutter across the land! These butterflies travel up to 7,500 miles across continents, one of the longest migrations of any insect. From the deserts of North Africa to the meadows of Europe, they flutter in search of food and breeding grounds. So raise your magnifying glasses in honor of these dedicated and delicate insects!

225. Watch out, the Pachycephalosaurus is charging through! With a head as tough as a bowling ball, this dino might have been the champion of the dinosaur head-butt. Think of it as the original hard-headed hero, always ready for a friendly tussle!

226. Dive into the Devonian seas for the Dunkleosteus, an armored fish with powerful jaws. Dominating the waters about 358 million years ago, its extinction marks the end of an era of armored marine predators. A jaw-dropping farewell to an ancient ocean ruler!

227. Flash a smile for the Masiakasaurus! The Masiakasaurus sported a unique set of teeth that pointed forward! These specialized teeth were likely for helping this fisher-dino snag his dinner straight out of the water. A resourceful dino with a snaggle-toothed grin!

228. Now, whisper, if you dare, the name Micropachycephalosaurus, a dino with a name that even a tongue-twister champion would have difficulty pronouncing! Despite its name suggesting something small, this dinosaur was anything but. Sporting a ginormous bony cranium, it was like a living helmet in a world of giants.

229. Grab your paraglider adventurers as we ride the thermals with the sandhill cranes. These birds embark on a 4,000-mile journey from their Arctic breeding grounds to warmer southern habitats. Flying high, they form large flocks, using thermal currents to travel vast distances with less energy. A smart bird that wings it most peculiarly!

230. Up into the air, we go! What a fabulous adventure to fly to new heights with the bar-headed goose as they soar over the Himalayas. These birds undertake one of the most extreme migrations, flying at altitudes over 29,000 feet to avoid mountain barriers. Their journey is a testament to their physiological adaptations to high altitudes. A bird with an altitude attitude!

231. Get low to the ground to meet the tiny Aquilops. The Aquilops was no bigger than your pet bunny but had a beak as sharp as an eagle's talon! This pint-sized dino was a mini mascot for the horned dinosaurs, proving that even in the age of giants, small can still be mighty!

232. Stalk the Pleistocene landscapes with the Saber-Toothed Tiger. Weighing up to 1,100 pounds, this predator with iconic elongated teeth hunted large herbivores. Around 10,000 years ago, it disappeared, possibly due to loss of prey and human hunting. A toothy goodbye to a fierce hunter!

233. Step into the lush Jurassic forests to meet the Stegosaurus, a dinosaur known for its distinctive row of bony plates and spiked tail. This herbivore, reaching up to 30 feet in length, used its tail spikes to defend itself against predators. The Stegosaurus vanished around 150 million years ago, likely due to drastic changes in climate and vegetation. A daring-looking dino, using its spikes only for defense!

234. Join me on a journey back to the Ice Age to meet the Woolly Mammoth! These shaggy giants, weighing up to 6 tons and standing 11 feet tall, roamed the icy plains. Sadly, around 4,000 years ago, they vanished due to climate change and human hunting. A frosty farewell to these furry behemoths!

235. Feel mighty with the Dreadnoughtus! This monstrosity among dinosaurs was so giant that it likely feared nothing! Once fully grown, it probably looked at other predators and thought, "Is that all you've got?" A true giant that walked the earth with confidence!

236. Join us for a meal with the Ampelosaurus, a dinosaur famous for its uniquely heart-shaped tailbone. This massive herbivore was quite the eater, chomping through roughly a ton of vegetation daily. Its distinctive tailbone aside, the Ampelosaurus was just a giant focused on its next leafy meal!

237. Stomp through Eurasia's Pleistocene forests with the Woolly Rhino. Adapted to the cold with a wooly coat and large horns, its extinction around 10,000 years ago marks the end of a hairy chapter in rhino history. A wooly wave goodbye to a frosty rhino!

238. Gaze upon the Gigantoraptor, a feathered and beaked giant of the Mesozoic era. This unique dino was thought to be the largest raptor of its time. A feathered reminder that sometimes dinosaurs look different than the scales we might expect!

239. Let's dive in and swim with the Spinosaurus! With a snout for sniffing out riverine snacks and feet that paddled through the Cretaceous currents with ease, this dino was a swimming sensation.

240. Peer over the deck to spot the Great Auk in the North Atlantic. This large, flightless seabird, similar to penguins, was hunted to extinction by the mid-19th century. A watery wave goodbye to a seabird lost in time!

241. Cruise the Yangtze River to remember the Baiji, a freshwater dolphin revered as the 'Goddess of the Yangtze.' Declared functionally extinct in 2006, it's a poignant reminder of the impact of industrialization on aquatic life. A silent farewell to riverine grace!

242. Dive in as we echo the majestic songs of the whales while they embark on their oceanic odyssey. These leviathans travel thousands of miles between feeding and breeding grounds. Humpback whales, for instance, migrate from polar waters to tropical or subtropical waters, a journey driven by the need to feed and breed. A magnificent creature that's not afraid to welcome the idea of migration!

243. Let's tiptoe through the forests of Mauritius in search of the Dodo. This unique, flightless bird lived peacefully until the 1600s when humans and invasive species arrived. Easy prey and unable to fly, the Dodo was hunted to extinction by the 1660s. A tragic end for our feathered friend!

244. Hoof stomping adventure ahead, adventurers! Migrate with the pronghorn across the North American plains. Their migration, covering up to 300 miles, is one of the longest land migrations in North America. They move in response to the seasons, seeking the best feeding and breeding conditions. A creature that shows no one hoofs it quite like the pronghorn!

245. Imagine the Mapusaurus, a gang of fearsome predators that might have hunted in packs. These dinosaurs worked together to take down giant prey, proving teamwork can make the dream work, even in the dinosaur world!

246. Stomp with me, explorers, 1,2,3! Stomping along the hidden paths in Africa, we might meet a majestic giant, the African forest elephant. These elephants move through the Congo Basin's dense forests, covering significant distances for food and water. Their migration patterns are less understood due to the dense forest cover. A story of a giant that never ceases to stop pounding the pavement!

247. Are you ready to meet the tiniest (non-bird) dino of all time? Say hello to the Fruitadens Haagarorum, tiny enough to dash beneath the feet of giants; it was the mouse among mammoths of the dinosaur world. This little dynamo proves that being small can still mean big adventures in a land of giants!

248. Unique as they come, the Balaur bondoc can teach us a thing or two about dexterity! With only two fingers on each hand, these were perfectly placed sickle claws! As the double-trouble terror of its time, this dino shows us that sometimes, having an extra edge (or claw) can make all the difference in the prehistoric playground!

249. Flashlights on, future paleontologists! As night fell, the Dilong might have prowled the shadows. This terrifying, tiny-eyed terror used the cloak of darkness to surprise its unsuspecting prey. This is a reminder that not all monsters need light to hunt!

250. Sail the North Pacific of the 18th century to meet the Steller's Sea Cow. This 30-foot-long gentle herbivore was hunted to extinction within 27 years of its discovery. A gentle giant's swift departure from the seas!

251. Swing with the Gigantopithecus, the most enormous ape ever. Roaming Southeast Asia's forests and subsisting on bamboo and fruit, this gentle giant's story ended about 100,000 years ago. A giant chapter closed in the primate storybook!

252. Is it a bird or a tiny raptor? Its appearance might be confusing, but the Microraptor was an itty bitty raptor with wings on all fours! Dinosaur experts debate its flying abilities, but it seems that gliding was as far as this creature flew! The dino was like an early experiment in prehistoric flight!

253. Let's leap across the land with the Stygimoloch. This fashionable dino has a name as sinister as its spiky skull! Once you see this cool creature's spiked head, it's easy to imagine that the Stugimoloch was the punk rocker of the Late Cretaceous, headbanging its way through the prehistoric scene.

254. Beware the Majungasaurus, the mysterious meat-eater of Madagascar! This dino was a bit of a puzzle, known for its unusual habit of nibbling on... other Majungasaurs! Imagine a dinosaur that didn't mind dining on its dino pals when snacks were scarce. A real-life mystery from the days of the dinosaurs!

255. Ready, set, fly! Soar swiftly with the Amur falcons on their extraordinary journey. These small raptors travel over 9,000 miles from their breeding grounds in Siberia to their wintering sites in southern Africa, one of the longest migrations of any bird of prey. A predatory bird known for its journey and the snacks it hunts along the way!

256. Tread through Carboniferous swamps with the Arthropleura, the largest land invertebrate. This 8.5-foot-long giant millipede's story, ending about 300 million years ago, is a reminder of the giants that once crawled the earth. A millipede's march into history!

ANIMAL ANTICS & ASTONISHMENTS

257. Shhh! If we go tiptoeing into our next adventure, we will find a snoozing sleepyhead. The Tufted Deer, native to China and Myanmar, has mastered the art of the power nap. Seated with heads resting on their bodies, they're ever-ready to spring into action. Their low profile? Nature's own camouflage amidst the forest underbrush!

258. Gather around curious minds. Are you ready to explore an animal home just as curious as we are? Take a journey to sub-Saharan Africa and tropical Asia with me, and you'll marvel at the weaverbirds' craftsmanship. These avian architects weave intricate, pouch-like nests from grasses, twigs, and leaves. You'll find entire neighborhoods in some trees, with multiple nests forming a cozy community. Nature's crafty animal apartments!

259. Flap your fins, adventurers, and let's mimic the dolphin, the sonar expert of the sea. They can emit up to 1,000 clicking noises per second and hear frequencies ten times above the human limit. This echolocation helps them find the smallest fish in complete darkness, up to 700 feet away. These flippered fish-eaters are always prepared to whip up a late-night snack.

260. Shh! We don't want to wake our next critter. Let's dive down to the ocean floor around the Galápagos Islands, where the Red-lipped Batfish takes beauty sleep to new depths. Buried in the sand, only its worm-like lips and eyes peek out. A snoozing creature waiting for a midnight snack!

261. Grab your scuba gear; we're diving deeper than deep! All the way down to the ocean floor of the Galápagos Islands. Here, the red-lipped batfish prefers to walk rather than swim, using its unique fins to emit a bright light to lure prey. A rare fish with an ultra-unique appearance!

262. Flap your wings, and we're off to Indonesia's treetops to peek at the red-knobbed hornbill's high-flying parenting! Mom Hornbill becomes a treehouse hermit, cocooning herself and her eggs in their nest while Dad's on fast-food duty. A dynamic duo of avian affection in the treetops!

263. Splash! Let's don our wetsuits and dive into the shimmering depths with the Three-spined Stickleback Fish. Dad fish are the castle keepers, building nests and guarding the future. A sparkling swirl of underwater vigilance and care.

264. Let's journey into the dense rainforests of Madagascar. Here, the aye-aye lemur taps away with its slender middle finger, listening intently for the telltale rustle of insects beneath the bark. Once it zeroes in, it skillfully extracts its prey, showcasing nature's ingenuity.

265. Come along and meet the ultimate water bottle warrior! Let's trudge through the desert sands with camels. These 'ships of the desert' have several adaptations for arid environments: their humps store fat (not water), they can drink 30 gallons in 15 minutes, and their nostrils and eyelashes keep out sand.

266. Onward to the grasslands of Central Asia! With their distinctive bulbous noses, the Saiga Antelopes use this solid snout to dig their ground beds. These depressions keep them hidden and are cozy enough for a quick nap. A unique herbivore with a crafty tool belt built right into their nose!

267. Hey, up here! Stretch your neck up high with the giraffes. They communicate using infrasound with frequencies below 20 Hz, which humans can't hear. This low-frequency communication allows them to coordinate with each other over long distances in the African savannah. A creature whose head stands high but who listens low.

268. Mud waders on, explorers! Let's venture into the wetlands of North America and discover the muskrat's lodges, which are made of vegetation and mud. These semi-aquatic rodents build homes in shallow water with hidden underwater entrances. It's a cozy, secretive abode where the muskrat can stay warm and dry amidst the surrounding water.

269. Quick, grab your climbing gear! We're scaling the treetops of Southeast Asia's rainforests. Among the leaves, the binturong, with its prehensile tail, swings from branch to branch, searching for a diverse meal ranging from fruits to birds' eggs. They certainly aren't eating those eggs, scrambled!

270. Drift through the skies with me and the baya weaver bird of South and Southeast Asia, and you'll be amazed by their hanging palaces. The males weave elaborate nests from leaves, showcasing their architectural prowess to find love. It's a delicate balance of form and function, where each strand is meticulously placed to create a secure, inviting home.

271. Buzz around various landscapes with me, and we may encounter the mud dauber wasps' tubular creations. Attaching their mud nests to walls, ceilings, or other surfaces, each cell of this nest holds a unique treasure: a paralyzed spider, a feast for the wasp's larvae. An insect that is buzzing with parental instinct!

272. Dive into the dense rainforests of Central and South America with me and encounter the leafcutter ants, the meticulous farmers of the insect world. They cultivate fungus gardens within their nests, using the leaves they meticulously cut and carry. It's a bustling underground world of agriculture, where each ant has a role in nurturing their fungal crops.

273. Buzz with me into the world of bees, where their compound eyes are adept at detecting ultraviolet light, allowing them to see patterns on flowers that are invisible to humans. These patterns, called nectar guides, direct them to the flower's sweet rewards.

274. Let's delve into the world of termites, where we'll discover nature's skyscrapers. These tiny builders erect towering mounds of soil, saliva, and feces. Some of these architectural wonders can reach up to 30 feet, complete with tunnels, chambers, and vents for climate control. Join me in marveling at these resourceful builder bugs!

275. Into the sky, we go! Here, we meet the Arctic tern, a migratory seabird with a minimalist approach to home-making. They carve out a simple, cozy nook by scraping a shallow underground depression. Whether on rocky shores or sandy areas, this bird proves that sometimes, simplicity is the ultimate sophistication.

276. Tune into the ultrasonic conversations of rodents. They communicate in high frequencies that are inaudible to humans, often as a defense mechanism against predators. Some species can emit and detect sounds up to 100 kHz in frequency. A silent squeak with purpose.

277. Let's camp in the forests of Africa and Asia! Where we might be lucky enough to see the Pangolins roll into view. These creatures are heavily endangered by poachers. Roll into perfect armored spheres, their scales interlock, and they create a fortress where they can dream without care. Nature's armored sleeping bag!

278. Let's soar along with the common swifts of Eurasia and Africa and be amazed by their aerial acrobatics. They create their nests using saliva as glue for sticks and feathers. These high-altitude homes are often hanging on cliffs or buildings. Nature's own sky-high apartments!

279. Time to dive deep again! In the Atlantic's abyss, the black swallower, a fish with quite the predatory prowess, shows off. With an expandable stomach, it can consume prey twice its size. Talk about an expansive appetite!

280. Strap on your snow boots and join us as we embark on an arctic adventure with the Polar Bears! Mother polar bears are the bearers of warmth in the frozen tundra, tenderly guiding their cubs in the art of Arctic survival. These cubs are with their mom for the first two and a half years of their life before venturing alone into the chilly wilds of the Arctic. A polar-full story of love and guidance in the cold!

281. Zoom over to our next speedy friend! In the vast African savannah, the sengi, also known as the elephant shrew, is always bustling about. This charming little mammal sports a snout reminiscent of an elephant's trunk, perfect for investigating insect hideouts and flipping leaves. When it's time to dine, the sengi cleverly uses its nose to dig tiny trenches, creating an insect trap. It then patiently waits to spring on its unsuspecting prey. A tiny detective with a nose for nature's treats!

282. Can you hop like a kangaroo? These creatures are always hopping and sparring, making them the bouncing boxers of Australia. Their unique way of moving is not just for speed; it's incredibly energy-efficient. Kangaroos can cover 25 feet in a single leap and reach speeds of over 35 mph, using less energy than if they walked!

283. Crouch down and prowl with me and the stealthy cats. Their whiskers, or vibrissae, are so sensitive they can detect changes in air currents as subtle as a breeze through a crack. These whiskers are rooted deeply in the skin and connected to the nervous system, helping them easily navigate tight spaces. Nature's built-in multitools.

284. Into the desert night, we go! The burrowing owl is on the prowl. It strategically places the feces around its burrow entrance using gathered animal dung. This gross but genius technique lures in dung beetles. Meanwhile, the owl is waiting and ready to attack its prey. A hoot of a hunting tactic!

285. Time to Bundle up and slip into an icy wonderland. Here, the Harp Seal mom gives the warmest cuddles to her babies. She keeps them close, nurturing and nursing her pups. A graceful glide of devotion and warmth in the frosty frontier!

286. Step into the underground world of East Africa with me, and you'll discover the naked mole-rats bustling cities. These creatures live in intricate tunnels and chambers and are led by a queen. It's a society so structured that it's called eusociality. A peculiar creature with an even more strange society!

287. Are you ready to meet a bird whose mouth acts like a thermostat? Then, fly with me to the rainforests to marvel at the toucan. Their large beaks aren't just for show; they help regulate body temperature. The beak rapidly adjusts blood flow, allowing toucans to release or conserve heat. A bird that feeds its own personal heater.

288. Form a line, team! On North America's lakes, the American white pelican uses teamwork to prepare for a feast. Working in unison, they strategically drive fish towards the shore, scooping them up with their large gular pouches. A perfectly synchronized team poised to outsmart their prey!

289. Are you ready to meet everyone's favorite pink bird? Then let's dance with the Greater Flamingo. Here, parents concoct a special crop of milk from their digestive tracts to feed their chicks. A shared dance of dining and devotion under the sun's spotlight. A fabulously feathered fable of these devoted parents and their babies!

290. Waders on, now follow me, explorers, into the shallow waters, where we can find the flamingo. Their upside-down beak is specially adapted for their feeding technique. They stir up mud with their feet, then use their beak to filter out food like shrimp and algae. A built-in flamingo filter!

291. Grab a snack and some water as we trek into the dense forests of Southeast Asia. We'll surely find the binturong, or bearcat, lounging high above in the trees. These nocturnal mammals make their beds on sturdy branches, curled up among the leaves. It's a lofty sanctuary where the binturong can rest in solitude and observe the world below. A high-risk hammock in the trees!

292. Wetsuits on deep sea divers! Dive with me alongside the seals. These clever creatures are using their whiskers to detect fish. Their whiskers can sense vibrations from fish swimming up to 600 feet away, making them incredibly adept hunters in murky waters. A slippery critter with a slick sense!

293. Join me in the silent flight of owls under the moon. Their eyes are not actual "eyeballs" but elongated tubes providing better depth perception and light gathering. They can spot a mouse over 200 feet away in near darkness, making them formidable nocturnal hunters. An inescapable predator poised to attack.

294. Dive into the deep with me, where sharks rule the waters with a sixth sense. They can detect electric fields as tiny as one-billionth of a volt, thanks to their ampullae of Lorenzini. This helps them locate prey, even those buried in sand, by sensing the electrical pulses every living creature emits. An electrifyingly toothy creature.

295. Follow me; let's dive in and swim to the coral reefs of the tropical oceans, and you'll be mesmerized by the clownfish's cozy homes within the sea anemones. These colorful swimmers form a symbiotic relationship with their stinging hosts, gaining protection while providing food. It's a harmonious underwater dance where each partner benefits from the other's presence.

296. Let's head to the Galapagos Islands, home of the vampire finch! When food is scarce, these birds have a spooky diet: they drink the blood of other birds! This creepy habit helps them get vital nutrients. Plus, they're known for sneaking into nests to eat eggs. It's a real-life nature mystery with the vampire finch as the star of this egg-citing story!

297. Bounce through the greenery with the jubilant Quokka and me. Here, mom quokkas are pouch-packed with love. As marsupials, these moms carry their joeys in pouches, cuddling them close until the babies are ready to peek out and explore the world! A joyful jump of affection hidden in this lush Australian landscape!

298. Let's scurry through the dark with rats. Their whiskers, or mystacial vibrissae, are highly sensitive to touch and can detect surface textures and breezes. These whiskers are so vital that a rat has difficulty navigating and capturing food without them.

299. Time to soar high with hawks, spotting prey from incredible distances. Their keen vision allows them to see eight times more clearly than the sharpest human eye. They can spot a rabbit moving almost a mile away. The birds with the built-in binoculars.

300. Grab your shovels! It's time to dig down with the burying beetle, where parenting is a meticulous art of transformation. They turn a bug carcass into a nursery and a buffet for their baby larvae. A fascinating foray into life's cycle and nature's nurturing beneath the leaves!

301. Join me on a trek through the southeastern United States, where we'll stumble upon the gopher tortoise's underground mansions. They dig burrows up to 40 feet long, providing shelter for themselves and over 350 other animal species, making them the ultimate hosts. Nature's innkeeper!

302. Flap your wings as fast as you can, everyone! Let's flutter with hummingbirds, the tiny dynamos of the sky. They can flap their wings up to 80 times per second, creating a humming sound. This rapid wing movement allows them to hover in place, a feat unique among birds.

303. Let's wander through the meadows of North America and stumble upon the prairie dogs' intricate burrow systems. These social rodents construct extensive underground towns with designated areas for nurseries, sleeping, and waste. It's a subterranean world of organization, where each tunnel serves a purpose in prairie dog society.

304. Flashlights on! In the Pacific's twilight zone, the pistol shrimp's oversized claw snaps shut, creating a jet of water so loud and forceful that it can stun or even kill its prey. Boasting what is considered one of the loudest sounds in the ocean, this small but mighty shrimp is a force to be reckoned with!

305. Are you ready to meet the eight-legged backpack buddies of the spider world? Then, let's creep through the moonlit world with the Wolf Spider. Here, dad spiders are the ultimate baby carriers, holding their future on their backs. A stealthy story of nocturnal nurturing and protection!

306. Grab your sun hats, water bottles, and pajamas! We're off to the deserts of Australia, where the Thorny Devil Lizard, with its spiky armor, has carved out a cozy burrow. Nestled beneath the sandy surface, it's the perfect escape from the scorching sun. A bedtime burrow for this beast!

307. Dive deep with whales, the giants of the ocean. Some species can dive over 2,000 feet deep and hold their breath for up to 90 minutes. These dives are crucial for feeding and navigating the ocean depths. A giant with a breathtaking ability.

308. Shh...did you feel that? Beneath our feet in North America's forests, the star-nosed mole prowls. Its unique nose, bristling with touch receptors, allows it to detect and devour prey in a flash. A nose that just knows!

309. Swing with me! In Borneo's treetops, the proboscis monkey munches on leaves rather than bananas! Its unique multi-chambered stomach houses a unique bacteria, which helps it digest tough cellulose or plant products. But here's a twist: this monkey's stomach can't break down the sugars in bananas or other fruits. This monkey gets his fill of greens!

310. Reach out with the octopuses, tasting their world with their suckers. Each sucker is packed with chemoreceptors, allowing them to taste everything they touch. This helps them distinguish between food and other objects in their environment. The octopus is the ocean's ultimate taste tester.

311. Zip up your parkas, adventurers! We're sliding over to the emperor penguins' icy kingdom. Weeee! Here, male penguins are the unsung heroes, juggling eggs on their toes in frigid temperatures while going on a food fast to keep their adorable future fluff balls safe. It's a frosty fable of penguin perseverance and parental love in the Antarctic!

312. Beware of the pit viper strike, which is fully equipped with a unique infrared vision. They have heat-sensing pits below their eyes, capable of detecting a temperature change as little as 0.003 degrees Celsius. This allows them to locate warm-blooded prey in complete darkness. Nature's high-powered and potent thermometer!

313. Be careful, explorers; our next creature is known to have a ferocious attitude! We might spy an alligator in the murky, mysterious marshlands if we look closely! Mother gators are nest-building champs, keeping a watchful eye on their precious eggs. Once the mini-gators hatch, it's a survival school with both parents as swamp-savvy instructors. A tale of toothy tenacity and marshland mastery!

314. Grab your hammocks and hang around with sloths, the leisurely loungers of the treetops. Their slow metabolism means they move at a languid pace, conserving energy. Sloths can take up to a month to digest a single meal! An animal that takes life at a leisurely pace!

315. Imagine being able to lift something 50 times your body weight? That's no imaginary task for the mighty ants. As the powerlifters of the insect world, they take the cake for the most vital insects, thanks to their strong exoskeletons. An incredible strength that is vital for their survival and colony building.

316. Hop along! In Australia's wetlands, the green tree frog awaits. It's on the hunt, devouring insects, spiders, and even smaller frogs. And when it's time, it recycles nutrients by consuming its shedding skin. A creature with a passion for recycling!

317. Waddle with me to the icy lands of the penguins. Their feathers are not just for show; they provide incredible insulation against the cold. Penguins have a layer of air trapped under their feathers, which can be as warm as 100°F, even in freezing temperatures. It is one of nature's most unique winter coats!

318. Next, we paddle into North American waterways, where we'll encounter beavers, the engineers of the animal kingdom. They craft dams from branches, mud, and stones, creating serene ponds. In the middle of those ponds, they build cozy homes that can only be accessed through secret underwater doors. Such Incredibly crafty critters!

319. Grab your shovels and dig deep with me into the world of star-nosed moles. Their unique star-shaped nose has over 25,000 sensory receptors, making it one of the most sensitive touch organs in the animal kingdom. This helps them to detect prey in just 8 milliseconds! This creature is the ultimate star of detection.

320. Shhh! Let's sneak into the bird world for a glimpse at the cuckoo's crafty childcare strategy. These avian actors trick other birds into raising their young in a feathery game of nest switcheroo. A story of slyness and survival in the sky-high nursery!

321. Race you to the next spot! On the ocean floor, the sunflower sea star speeds by. It's a speedy predator with up to 24 arms, devouring everything from clams to other sea stars. A creature that is a star predator!

322. Up, up, up we climb, through the towering trees of the rainforests, to discover the orangutans' treetop havens. These intelligent primates weave branches and foliage to create comfy nests each night. High above the ground, they find solace in their leafy beds, shielded from predators and the elements. Talk about an ultra-high bunk bed!

323. Can you taste the air, explorers? Snakes certainly can! So slither with me as we discover how snakes can taste the air. Their forked tongues collect airborne particles and transfer them
to the Jacobson's organ in the mouth, allowing them to 'taste' the air, track their prey, or navigate their environment.

324. Sleepily swing up with me to the treetops of Southeast Asia! Here, the Tarsiers, one of the smallest primates in the world, are catching some zzzs. Clinging to vertical branches, they tuck their heads between their legs, a perfect hideaway from daytime predators. A peaceful predator-proof pose!

325. Brr explorers, it's time to pull on those big fluffy coats! In the Arctic, seals showcase their diving skills. Some species can hold their breath for up to two hours, diving deep in search of food. That's like having a scuba tank built into your body!

326. Time to dive, once again, into the ocean! In the Atlantic's depths, the green sea slug has a secret. It's one of the few animals that can photosynthesize, turning sunlight into energy, just like plants. A slug with a knack for adaptation!

327. Next, let's slather on the sunscreen as we amble across the African savanna with elephants. Here, the all-knowing matriarch leads family ties as strong as their trunks. Together, they nurture and shield their young in a majestic journey of wisdom and wanderlust.

328. Ready, aim, splash! In Southeast Asia's clear waters, the sharpshooting archerfish takes aim. It spits water jets at insects above, knocking them down for a tasty treat. These accurate archers can shoot streams up to 10 feet. That would be similar to a human spitting on the top of a telephone pole!

329. Let's move on to pastures in Europe to graze with a creature you might recognize! That's right, the cow! In their unique four-chambered stomach, they ferment their food, helping them extract essential nutrients from rigid plant material. Nature's show of complexity and internal innovation!

330. Do you hear that sound, adventurers? Elephants are afoot! As we embark on a journey to the vast landscapes of Africa, we spot majestic African elephants. Instead of intricate nests, these gentle giants use their mighty trunks and tusks to dig a shallow depression in the ground. It's their way of creating a temporary, comfy resting spot, shielded from the sun and potential threats.

331. Let's flutter along the flower garden with butterflies as they taste with their feet. Their feet have chemoreceptors that can detect the right host plants for laying eggs. This ensures their caterpillars have the right food source, which is crucial for survival.

332. Venture with me into the realms of Europe and Asia, and you'll be captivated by the artistry of the wasp spider. Crafting orb-shaped webs adorned with a unique zigzag pattern called a stabilimentum, this spider's creation is not just structural but also a masterclass in camouflage.

333. Creep into the world of spiders, where each web strand is a vibration sensor. Spiders can detect the type of prey caught in their web based on the frequency of vibrations, helping them distinguish between a meal and a mere leaf.

334. Let's stroll along sandy beaches, where we'll witness the artistry of sand bubbler crabs. As they forage, they craft small, spherical sand pellets, arranging them in mesmerizing patterns around their burrows. It's nature's own sand art, refreshed with every tide.

335. Venture into the South American grasslands and find the anteater, nature's insect vacuum! Its long, sticky tongue is perfect for slurping up thousands of ants and termites daily. This unique adaptation allows it to feast on a wiggly and plentiful diet. A true master of munching on the move!

336. Hold your noses, team! Let's paddle through the Amazon, where the "stinkbird," or hoatzin, gives away its presence. It ferments leaves in its crop, which emits a unique odor. An animal that lives up to its name!

337. Watch your head! In the Himalayas, the bearded vulture drops bones from high in the sky, shattering them to feast on the nutritious marrow inside the bones. A rain you definitely don't want on your parade!

338. Take a journey with me to the icy landscapes of Antarctica and witness the emperor penguins' communal living. Without a physical structure to call home, they huddle together for warmth. It's a living, breathing fortress against the freezing winds and temperatures. A creature that uses the power of unity to survive!.

339. Flit through the forests with me! In Thailand, one of the world's smallest mammals, the bumblebee bat, hovers near flowers. Its elongated tongue extracts nectar, playing a vital role in pollination. A tiny creature with a mighty appetite!

340. Fly high, explorers! Over Southeast Asia, the helmeted hornbill is on a fruit-gathering mission. Its sharp beak skewers fruit, catching it expertly in its throat pouch. Nature's high-flying acrobat with an edible trick!

341. Hop into the world of the Surinam toad, where moms are living nurseries! Their backs become a safe haven for eggs, which hatch into tadpoles and tiny toads. A leap into the life cycle and a tale of amphibian awe in the aquatic world. Nature's natural baby carrier!

342. Climb aboard our cozy cruise ship to meet another creature! In the icy waters of the Arctic, you'll find the male Narwhal, often called the "unicorn of the sea." Their tusks point to the sky as they drift in a vertical slumber, conserving energy in the deep blue. Nature's compass, pointed straight at the stars!

343. Next, we hop over to the deserts of the southwestern United States and marvel at the cactus ferruginous pygmy owl's unique dwellings. These tiny owls make their homes within the arms of saguaro cacti, finding refuge in the spiny giants. It's a prickly haven where the owls can have a literal birds-eye view!

344. Blow bubbles with the humpback whales! In the Pacific, these crafty hunters are creating a net of bubbles. These bubble nets trap fish, allowing them to feast with ease. A showcase of incredible ingenuity from an exceptionally magnificent creature!

345. Grab your detective hats, and let's trail with the bloodhounds. Their sense of smell is so refined they can follow a scent trail for over 130 miles and even detect smells up to 300 hours old. They have about 300 million scent receptors, compared to a human's 5 million!

346. Let's head down under into the world of the platypus of Eastern Australia and Tasmania men and be intrigued by their riverside burrows. These unique mammals dig lengthy tunnels along the banks, with a cozy chamber at the end for resting and raising their young. It's a quirky hidden retreat for an extra quirky animal!

347. Keep those hats on! Still venturing through the deserts of Mongolia and China, we stumble upon the Long-eared Jerboas! These restful rodents have crafted intricate burrows, their secret hideaway from the desert's heat and prying eyes. Multiple chambers? Check. Multiple exits? Check. Ultimate desert fortress? Absolutely!

348. Put on your most colorful glasses and join me in marveling at the mantis shrimp. Their eyes can see from ultraviolet to polarized light, boasting 16 types of color-receptive cones, while humans have only 3. This allows them to detect predators and prey in the most vibrant colors imaginable.

349. Are you ready for a sand-tastic journey? Then, grab your gear and scurry through the sands with the meerkats. Everyone chips in to raise the young in this sandy society, from babysitting to teaching survival skills. A sandy saga of community and care in the critter kingdom!

350. Plunge into the deep with me and our friends, the elephant seals. They use echolocation to hunt in the ocean's pitch-black depths, diving as deep as 5,000 feet and holding their breath for up to two hours while searching for food. A patient predator prowling through the dark ocean!

351. Ready, set, run, adventurers! Race with me alongside the cheetahs, the fastest land animals. They can accelerate from 0 to 60 mph in just 3 seconds! Their flexible spine, long legs, and non-retractable claws make them the ultimate sprinters. A creature built to be the ultimate speed hunter.

352. Let's make our way to the savannas of Africa! Here, you'll be enchanted by the meerkats' subterranean realms. These social mammals live in complex burrow systems with multiple entrances and chambers. It's a maze beneath the sun-baked earth where the meerkats find shade and safety in numbers.

353. Splash! Dive deep to dance with the seahorses, where dads do the extraordinary – they give birth! Watch these graceful gents swirl and twirl in an underwater ballet of birth and bonding. A mesmerizing marine marvel of role reversal!

354. Let's journey to Australia, where we'll witness the Australian fairy wrens' house-building skills. The male, ever the eager builder, crafts dome-shaped nests with side entrances. He often presents multiple options, letting the female pick her favorite for laying eggs. The real estate agent of the bird world!

355. Look around, explorers. Do you see that? Our next creature glows in the dark! In the Antarctic's icy waters, the krill lure in their prey with bioluminescence. Emitting a blue-green light, they attract small fish, capturing them with their front legs. Quite the skilled fishermen!

356. Do you feel that? That's the ground trembling because of the mighty elephants. They communicate using infrasound, with frequencies as low as 14 Hz, which can travel over 6 miles. These low-frequency rumbles are heard and felt through the elephants' sensitive feet and trunks.

357. Let's grab a flight to Europe, and you'll encounter the European hornet's multi-story homes. They construct paper-like nests using chewed wood and saliva, often tucked away in tree hollows or buildings. These nests house hundreds of hornets across layers of hexagonal cells. A fantastic fortress that holds their buzzing metropolis together!

358. As we buzz over to the realm of honeybees, prepare to be in awe of their geometric genius. They sculpt hexagonal nests called honeycombs from beeswax, which serve as pantries for honey and pollen and nurseries for their young. You'd be amazed at what a bee can do!

359. Let's hop into the twilight with a fan favorite, the frog! Their eyes contain many rod cells, perfect for low-light conditions. This allows them to spot insects and predators even on the darkest nights, making every evening a potential feast.

360. Drift into dreamland with the currents along the coasts of Australia, where the Leafy Sea Dragons, relatives of seahorses, are masters of disguise. Even in sleep, they're camouflaged, blending seamlessly with the swaying seaweed. Nature's protective pajamas!

361. Spread your wings, and let's navigate with pigeons. They have iron-rich cells in their beaks that allow them to detect the earth's magnetic field, aiding in their incredible homing ability. They can return to their nests from distances as far as 1,300 miles away. A common bird with a non-so-common built-in compass.

362. Trek into the rainforest and marvel at the Strawberry Poison Dart Frog with me. Among this species, the dads stand guard over eggs while moms taxi tadpoles on their backs, seeking the perfect puddle. A vibrant vignette of amphibian affection and dedication in the jungle that's always ready to hop to it in their parenting roles.

363. Floatation devices were deployed, explorers, as we paddled gently along so as not to disturb the Giant Water Bug. These insect dads are excellent guardians, balancing their future offspring on their backs until hatching. A serene story of paternal protection and love on the water's surface!

364. Fasten your capes, young adventurers, and soar with me alongside the incredible bats! Using echolocation, they emit sound waves that bounce back from objects, allowing them to navigate in complete darkness. Isn't it wild that a bat can emit up to 20,000 echolocation pulses per minute while hunting?

365. Climb high, fellow bird watchers! In New Zealand, the kakapo, a flightless parrot, strips bark away from trees to access the nutrient-rich cambium layer, making the most of its buffet. These not-so-picky parrots also munch on roots, seeds, fruit, moss, and insects. That's the opposite of a picky eater!

366. Let's explore an animal home that is an incredibly cozy den in a very harsh climate! Through the rocky landscapes of the Himalayas, and encounter the snow leopard's solitary hideaways. These elusive cats find refuge among the cliffs and crevices, blending seamlessly with their surroundings. It's a secluded haven where the snow leopard can survey its mountainous realm undisturbed.

BIZARRE BIOLOGY: HUMAN & BEYOND

367. Hello there! You've brought your lab coat; we'll need it to explore the body's 'spit factory.' That's right, your body has its own production line! Our bodies churn out 1 to 1.5 liters of saliva daily! This isn't just for show; saliva plays a pivotal role in breaking down food and defending against bacteria, ensuring every bite you take is well-lubricated and ready for digestion!

368. The race is on! The nail growth race that is. Fingernails are the ultimate sprinters versus the slow and steady toenails. Who will win? Fingernails! They come dashing into the race three times faster than the toenails. So, if you're waiting for those toenails to catch up, grab a snack; it will be a while!

369. Are you ready to learn about a memory that is as amazing as they come? Time to learn about eidetic memory! After a brief exposure, these fascinating individuals can recall images, sounds, or objects with astonishing precision. It's like having a magical camera in your brain, capturing every detail of the world around you!

370. Next, on our time-hopping journey, we navigate the crowded streets of 19th-century Boston, where the silent threat of Neisseria meningitidis looms. This bacterium caused meningitis, a severe illness that many faced without our current defenses. But now, thanks to medical advancements like vaccines, we've turned the tide against this old foe. It's a testament to how far we've come in protecting our health and securing a brighter, healthier future.

371. Feel the ancient energy? We're standing atop rocks from 3.4 billion years ago, which tell tales of earth's earliest days. These stones reveal stories of bacterial life forms, such as ancient Archaebacteria that thrived in extreme conditions like hot springs and deep-sea vents. These hardy pioneers set the stage for the diverse world of life we see today!

372. Aaa-aaaa-aaaachoooo! A sneeze isn't just a sneeze; it's a high-speed chase! Every time you go "Achoo!", the air whooshes out at nearly 100 miles per hour. It's like your body's way of launching unwanted invaders out, ensuring your nasal passages remain a no-fly zone for dust and germs. So be sure to grab a tissue, and you can keep those invaders from spreading
around tiny virus particles!

373. Strap on your goggles and step into the lab! Here, phages, microscopic viral gladiators, are taking center stage. These tiny champions tackle troublesome bacteria, especially those that resist our antibiotics, from the inside out. With such powerful allies, we're ready to face even the toughest bacterial bullies!

374. Let's dig our hands into the soil and feel the world beneath! Pseudomonas aeruginosa, a crafty bacteria, lurks not just on the earth but on everyday surfaces, too. It's a sneaky little critter known to cause various infections, especially when it enters wounds or the lungs. But with a bit of handwashing magic and some trusty knowledge, we can keep our dance with these microscopic maestros in perfect harmony!

375. Ready, set, go! Time to sprint alongside the marathon runners! These endurance experts can complete a 26.2-mile race in just over two hours. It's a symphony of determination, training, and physical prowess, a dance of muscles and mind pushing towards the finish line!

376. Let's make a splash at the next stop of our microscopic adventure! At a pool party, amidst the laughter and splashes, be cautious of the uninvited guest: the Norovirus. This contagious rascal can turn a fun day into a tummy turmoil fest. So remember, wash those hands before you dine!

377. Brrr! Grab your winter coat and brace yourselves to meet the icemen! These cold warriors can endure freezing temperatures that would make a polar bear shiver. It's a blend of meditation, breathing techniques, and sheer will, allowing them to walk through winter wonderlands in shorts!

378. If you thought birds were all sweet songs and pretty feathers, meet the fulmar. With its sharp eyes and sturdy wings, this seabird has a unique way of saying, "Back off!" When danger is near, it can projectile vomit an oily substance up to several feet away. It's a clear message: mess with the fulmar, and you're in for a nasty surprise!

379. Nature's recycling program has a star participant: the treehopper. With its ornate body shape, this insect secretes a sweet "honeydew" liquid. This sugary treat helps it attract ants, which protects the treehopper from predators. A sweet deal for both parties!

380. Microscopes out as we explore the good, the bad, and the ugly world of bacteria! You may imagine that bacteria is always a villainous foe. However, in this story, they are the heroes of our digestive system! Good bacteria are essential to ensuring our digestive systems remain well-oiled machines. From breaking down food to keeping harmful invaders at bay, they're always here to save the day!

381. Neuroplasticity, the marvel of our brain, ensures we are always ready to create a new masterpiece. It's our brain's wondrous ability to rewire and adapt based on new experiences and learning. As you take in the world around you or experience thoughts—your brain is busy rewiring itself based on this new information. Think of it as having an in-house architect who is always ready to remodel and renovate!

382. Let's hop back into the new millennium, the year 2003! In a tiny water droplet, scientists stumbled upon the Mimivirus, a giant among viruses. It's so huge, it's almost as big as bacteria! Found inside a water-loving amoeba, this virus made everyone rethink the tiny world of germs. Imagine finding a whale in your fishbowl!

383. Alright, time-travelers! Now we're zipping to Paris in the year 1881. Amidst the glow of gas lamps, the legendary scientist Louis Pasteur is hard at work in his lab. After years of tireless research on the rabies virus, he unveiled this game-changing vaccine. With his genius, a once fearsome bite turned into a tale of victory. Onward to more discoveries!

384. Onward to the super-recognizers! With their facial recognition prowess, they can remember faces they've glimpsed once, even years ago. It's like having a mental gallery of every face they've ever seen, making them invaluable in many career fields!

385. Hair today, gone tomorrow, but fear not! For every strand that says goodbye, there's another to take its place. So, even if you spot some hairs on your brush, remember the next star of this hairy show is always ready to be the next shining star!

386. Skip, hop, jump, and leap with the parkour practitioners! These urban ninjas navigate through concrete jungles with a grace that would make a cat envious. It's a dance of agility, strength, and precision, turning the city into a pouncing playground!

387. Climbing back into our Time Machine, we are whisked away to the bustling bathhouses of Ancient Rome. Where we encounter Tinea, the fungus responsible for causing ringworm. This common skin infection is easily spread in communal areas. But today, with our knowledge and hygiene, we can easily fend off this ancient adversary.

388. Imagine an organ with the power to control every function of your body. That's right. Your brain is the literal powerhouse of your body! It even generates enough electricity to power a small light bulb. This energy helps your brain send messages to different body parts, allowing you to think, move, and feel.

389. Pushing through crowded town squares, the bacteria Staphylococcus aureus silently spreads. Present in many, it can lead to infections, oozing blisters, and gastrointestinal symptoms, but it only strikes where it finds an opening! With cleanliness and care, we can coexist with this omnipresent observer.

390. Teeth, the guards of our oral realm, stand at attention, ensuring every bite is mashed to perfection, every word is crystal clear, and every smile is a radiant beacon of joy! Beyond their aesthetic appeal, they play a crucial role in our overall health, from aiding digestion to helping shape our speech. Say cheese!

391. Craft dreamscapes with the lucid dreamers! These dream weavers can control their nocturnal journeys, much like having a mental video game controller! They can shape and explore the realms of their minds, knowing they are dreaming. It's like being the creator of your own nightly adventure!

392. Bones here, bones there, bones everywhere! Let's explore the skeleton, boasting 206 bones; the skeleton is a grand display of architecture, with each bone intricately designed and methodically placed. It provides the foundation for our bodies and allows us to run, walk, jump, and dance to the rhythm of life!

393. Grab your swim fins and goggles; we're diving into another watery adventure! But be careful; lurking in the shadows is Cryptosporidium, a sneaky little parasite. It can journey to our intestines if swallowed, causing some not-so-fun tummy troubles. So, adventurers. Always ensure our swimming spots are sparkling clean.

394. Come along, adventurers, as we travel the Silk Road. This is where traders from the East and West exchanged not only goods and commodities but also tales of the Shigella bacteria! This sneaky pathogen caused shigellosis, leading to many a traveler's tales of woe. But today, we can keep this bacterium at bay with clean water and food. Talk about an ancient traveler's nightmare!

395. Night owls meet the oilbird or guácharo. This nocturnal bird, native to the caves of South America, has a unique approach to waste. Instead of the usual droppings, it secretes a waxy substance, which doubles up as building material for its nests. Talk about upcycling!

396. Sweat might seem like nature's pungent perfume, but the real culprits behind that distinct aroma are the tiny bacteria partying on your skin. They feast on the body's sweat, turning it into quite a fragrant affair. So, when you're breaking a sweat, that smell is only the body's bacteria having a celebratory feast!

397. The liver is not just an organ; it's quite the superhero! Even if it's down and out, with 75% of it damaged, it can heal and regenerate itself! Toxins don't stand a chance with your super-liver at work!

398. All aboard the Earwax Express, explorers! Truck along, and you'll find an ooey-gooey and orange substance that serves one primary purpose: to protect our ears! This guardian of the eardrums acts as a sticky barrier to ensure no unwanted guests like dust or bacteria crash the party.

399. Dive into the abyss with the free divers! These aquatic adventurers plunge into the ocean's depths without a breathing apparatus. It's a dangerous journey into the unknown, a dance with the deep blue, pushing the boundaries of human capabilities!

400. Imagine a factory that produces 2 million products every second. That's our bone marrow for you! Our bone marrow churns out oxygen-carrying red blood cells, infection-fighting white blood cells, and the platelets that control bleeding when we get injured, all at lightning speed. Bone marrow is the powerhouse that keeps our body oxygenated, healthy, and safe!

401. Time to roll over to greet the European rollerbird. With its vibrant blue feathers, this feathered friend believes in fighting stink with stink. When threatened, it regurgitates a foul-smelling orange liquid. It's a clear message: mess with the roller, and you're in for a stinky surprise!

402. Dive deep, and you just might meet the ocean quahog clam. This is different from your average clam. When it feels threatened, it lights up the ocean with bioluminescent mucus, ensuring any predator gets a light show that they won't forget. A clam with a glow-up!

403. Add yourself to the wild world of math! Here, we meet mental calculators! These numerical wizards can solve intricate mathematical problems in their heads faster than you can say "calculator." It's like having a supercomputer in their brains, crunching numbers, and solving equations in the blink of an eye!

404. All aboard the Time-Travel Express! Let's cautiously explore the streets of ancient Greece and Rome. Here, anthrax, caused by the bacteria Bacillus anthracis, is a hot topic of discussion. But in our time, thanks to antibiotics, we've got this ancient menace under control.

405. Next, let's dance through the harmonious realm of absolute pitch! These musical maestros can recognize or reproduce any musical note without external reference. It's a symphony in the brain, where every note dances in perfect harmony, a gift believed to be a blend of genetics and early musical training!

406. Say cheese! Did you know it takes about 17 muscles to create your awesome smile but around 43 muscles to make a frown? So, keep smiling and spread some cheer – it's easier!

407. Ah, the nose! Did you know your nose can discern between an astounding 50,000 scents? Whether it's the earthy aroma of a forest after rain or the scrumptious scent of a freshly baked pie, the nose ensures we're constantly immersed in a world of aromatic wonders.

408. Down here in the soil, an elusive fungus called Histoplasma capsulatum lurks. This sneaky fungus can cause histoplasmosis, especially if you're near bird or bat droppings. Adventurers, always be wary of where you tread!

409. Ever thought a handshake was a strange way to say hello? With its distinctive black and white coat, the Malayan tapir takes greetings to a whole new level. By sniffing and analyzing the aroma of each other's dung, they can tell a fellow tapir's age, relationship status, and even their gender. It's like reading a biography with just a whiff!

410. Have you hydrated today? If not, this is your sign to grab a glass of water! It's so important! Over half of our bodies are made up of this lovely drink. Our internal reservoir ensures that every cell is nourished, every function sails smoothly, and we remain the epitome of vitality. So, drink up!

411. If you thought skunks were the only stink masters, meet the garter snake. This colorful reptile, often found in gardens, has a secret weapon: a noxious-smelling liquid. This helps keep any threat at bay, and it's often mistaken for the aroma of a skunk. A snake with a smelly strategy!

412. Buried deep in the archives of ancient apothecaries, tales of Clostridium difficile tell of this known troublemaker. Linked to various gastrointestinal symptoms, this bacterium was a challenge. But in modern times, we've tamed this old foe with advanced healthcare settings!

413. Look around as we gaze through the eyes of the tetrachromats! These color connoisseurs can see a spectrum of colors beyond our imagination. It's like having an extra paintbrush to color the world, allowing them to perceive a myriad of shades invisible to the average eye!

414. Next up is the immune system! The real superhero of your body. It is constantly working to fight off germs and to keep you healthy. It uses white blood cells to defend your body against harmful invaders like bacteria, viruses, and other microscopic troublemakers. Thanks to these heroic helpers, your body can stay strong and energetic!

415. Meet the peccary, nature's version of a stink bomb. This wild pig look-alike, often found in groups in the Americas, has a potent trick to deter threats. When danger is near, it emits a powerful odor from a gland on its back. This scent is so strong that humans can detect it from a distance, ensuring any predator thinks twice before approaching.

416. Leap into the lush rainforests to meet the red-eyed tree frog, a dazzling amphibian with a unique way of staying hydrated. Instead of sipping from a pond, this frog absorbs moisture right through its skin like a living sponge! And when it's time to eliminate the excess, it releases a special milky stream. This keeps the frog refreshed and ready for its next big jump. Talk about a natural hydration hero!

417. Speeding right along, we encounter the speed readers! These literary lightning bolts can consume words at a rate that would make a hummingbird's wings seem slow. Imagine absorbing entire novels in the time it takes most people to finish a chapter, all while understanding every twist and turn of the plot!

418. Take a deep breath. And now, let it out. Seems like a simple task, doesn't it? However, there is nothing simple about this extraordinary process of filling our lungs with oxygen. And did you know that your lungs are much larger than they look? If you lay out your lungs, the surface area of all the lobules and alveoli is almost as big as half a tennis court!

419. Popcorn at the movies is great, but have you actually smelled a binturong? This creature, often called the "bearcat," marks its territory with a musky secretion that smells oddly like your favorite movie snack. Nature declares, "This is my domain, and I'm here to enjoy the show!"

420. Let's dive deep into the cosmos of our cellular makeup. Here you'll find trillions of cells, each playing its part in sustaining life. From the tiny red blood cells delivering oxygen to the large nerve cells transmitting signals, every cell in our body is a shining star in the universe that is us.

421. Green might be the color of envy, but the Australian green tree frog wears it for defense. This vibrant amphibian, often found in gardens and homes, secretes a sticky, white substance when threatened. This gooey barrier ensures it's off the menu for hungry predators.

422. Think salt is just for seasoning your fries? Meet the giant petrel, a bird with an impressive wingspan and a unique problem: too much salt! Living in the ocean means a lot of salty meals, but no worries — this clever bird has its own built-in salt filter. It sneezes out excess salt in a briny spray, keeping itself healthy and ready for its next ocean adventure. Talk about a natural salt shaker!

423. What gets us on the move? It's our muscles, of course! With over 600 muscles, our body is like an orchestra, and every step we take is a symphony with multiple muscles working together to create the beauty of motion. Over 200 of these muscles ensure our walk is graceful, our run is swift, and our dance is lively.

424. Do you smell that? Someone's cooking! Amidst the sizzle and aroma of bustling kitchens, chefs are on high alert! Listeria monocytogenes might be lurking nearby. This mischievous bacterium can cause listeriosis, giving you more than a tummy ache. Ensure your food is fresh and well-cooked to keep this unwelcome guest at bay.

425. Follow me to explore the grand bazaars along ancient trade routes! Here, merchants spoke of a flu-like virus called Enterovirus. This virus caused many illnesses, from hand, foot, and mouth disease to viral meningitis. Today, with hygiene and awareness, we keep these old-world viruses under control.

426. Next, we're plunging into the icy depths of Siberia! Here, frozen in time, is the Pithovirus sibericum, a 30,000-year-old GIANT virus. Even after millennia, this ancient behemoth can still infect amoebas. It's like a living time capsule, teaching scientists about the resilience of viruses.

427. We'll need all the brain power we can get to learn about the incredible power of the human brain! Your brain has lightning-fast prowess, making it an ultimate tech marvel. It can perform up to a thousand fundamental processes every second, ensuring that you're perpetually synced, able to process vast arrays of information, and react in nanoseconds!

428. Fasten your seatbelts as we soar back to ancient civilizations! From the bustling streets of Rome to the grand palaces of India, the chatter of leprosy caused by Mycobacterium leprae was everywhere. But fear not, time travelers! In our present day, this old tale has a new ending – one of hope and healing, all thanks to modern medicine.

429. Now, shrink down with me to the size of a speck, and let's embark on a fantastic voyage through the human tummy! Here, we'll meet a long-time resident, Helicobacter pylori, often called 'H. pylori' for short. This tiny tenant has been living in the bellies of humans for 60,000 years! While it sometimes gets a bit rowdy by causing ulcers, most of the time, it's just chilling out, enjoying the cozy environment.

430. Hello! Bonjour! Hola! Join me in conversation with the language savants! These linguistic maestros can pick up languages with an ease that leaves most of us in awe. It's like having a universal translator in their brains, allowing them to understand the tapestry of human communication in multiple tongues!

431. Ring-a-ding! Let's head to Philadelphia, home of the Liberty Bell. The year is 1976, and there's more than just the bell making noise. A mysterious outbreak has grabbed headlines, leading scientists to uncover the culprit: the Legionella pneumophila bacteria. It's the sneaky agent behind Legionnaire's disease. With a name like that, it sure sounds like a super-villain, doesn't it?

432. When you think of flakes, do you think of snow? When I think of flakes, future scientists, I think of snow and the incredible regeneration capabilities of the human body! Skin flakes are like the diligent librarians of the body, archiving old cells and ushering in the new. With 30,000 to 40,000 skin cells saying goodbye every minute, a fresh batch of flakes is always ready to face the world!

433. Hippos have their own SPF solution. They ooze a "blood sweat," a red, oily substance that protects them from the sun and has antibiotic properties. This secretion helps these giants stay healthy while basking in the sun, and it's not blood at all but a unique skin moisturizer.

434. Venture to see the vast lakes and streams of the world, but don't drink the water! Lurking in certain waterways is a microscopic parasite called Giardia. This tiny invader can cause giardiasis, a severe gastrointestinal illness. Let this be a reminder, explorers, to ensure your water sources are properly clean and treated!

435. Wandering Victorian London streets, the bacterium Haemophilus influenzae was an invisible threat, causing ailments from pneumonia to meningitis. But today, with vaccines and treatments, the foggy tales of old London are just that. Foggy tales.

436. Feeling a little embarrassed? Butterflies in your stomach? Blushing is to blame! When you blush, it's not just your cheeks that turn red — the lining of your stomach blushes too! It's all because of the increased blood flow when you feel embarrassed or excited.

437. Gathering around rustic kitchens, stories of Campylobacter were shared. Responsible for many food poisoning disasters, it lurked in undercooked poultry and unpasteurized milk. Today, our culinary prowess ensures this guest doesn't crash our meals.

438. Tooooot! Excuse me! It seems it's time to talk about a musical instrument we all play, sometimes silently, sometimes... not so much. Passing gas! It's like our body's way of playing the trumpet. Up to 23 times a day, in fact. It's just the symphony of digestion, ensuring no unwanted air overstays its welcome.

439. Next, we're blasting off into the cosmos in search of 'Conan the Bacterium,' or Deinococcus radiodurans! Discovered in a can of irradiated meat, this tiny marvel stunned scientists with its resistance to radiation. So much so that they sent it to space to test its mettle. Amidst the stars, it showcased life's incredible resilience and adaptability!

440. Let's wade into shimmering freshwater habitats and explore the vibrant world of Cyanobacteria. These tiny organisms gave the earth its first significant breath of oxygen 2.4 billion years ago and continue their hard work today, contributing to nearly a third of our planet's oxygen! Talk about a breath of fresh air!

441. The bombardier beetle is about to blow your mind! No, really! This crafty insect, found in grasslands worldwide, unleashes a fiery, hot, and pungent chemical spray from its abdomen, reaching temperatures nearly 100°C when threatened. This chemical reaction is so intense it can even produce a small explosion! Talk about a beetle with a bang!

442. Did you know that your hair retains the history of everything in your bloodstream? Each strand is a chronicle narrating tales of our past and present. Hair (as well as hair loss) can also tell us a great deal about our overall health and age. Hair can act as a looking glass into our past and future.

443. Ever wonder how our stomach acid can digest food without digesting our stomach itself? Imagine your stomach is a medieval castle with a moat. It rebuilds its biological protective barrier every two weeks, ensuring the acidic dragons don't attack the castle walls. Without this mucus moat, our stomachs would be in a real medieval battle!

444. Venture into the dense forests of South America, and you may encounter the capuchin monkey. These intelligent primates, with their expressive faces and nimble fingers, have a unique way of dealing with pests. They crush millipedes and rub the millipedes' foul-smelling excretions all over their fur. Staying smelly and stylish!

445. Tonsil stones might not sound fun, but they're usually relatively harmless. Formed from a mix of mucus, bacteria, and dead cells, they might cause a tickle or two in our throat. But fret not; it's just a sign that your body's continually and thoroughly cleaning itself to help you stay in tip-top shape.

446. Before fancy perfume shops, the African civets were the original perfumers. With their sleek fur and sharp eyes, these nocturnal creatures whip up civetone, a musky aroma that's been the secret behind many perfumes for centuries. This secretion, once harvested, ensures the allure lasts all day.

447. Echoing through medieval European monasteries, monks transcribed tales of Bordetella pertussis, the bacterium behind whooping cough. Their writings told of severe coughing fits. Today, vaccines have helped to turn the tide against this ancient adversary!

448. Sniffle sniffle! Ever wondered what makes your nose runny? Mucous! This wonderfully icky fluid is the unsung hero of our respiratory tract. Our body produces approximately a liter daily, ensuring that dust and debris can have a smooth sail out of our bodies! Tissue, anyone?

449. Don't let the millipede's many legs distract you; it has another trick up its sleeve. These ancient arthropods, marching around for over 400 million years, have a secret smelly weapon. When danger is near, they release a toxic and foul-smelling chemical. It's their way of saying, "Not today!"

450. Let's venture into the labyrinth of hyperthymesia, where we find individuals who can recall the most minute details of their lives with extraordinary accuracy. It's like having a personal time machine, allowing them to revisit every day of their lives, experiencing every emotion and every sensation once again!

451. You'll appreciate the stinkbug's tactics if you like your personal space. This shield-shaped bug doesn't believe in subtlety. Feeling threatened, it releases a pungent liquid from special glands, ensuring any intruder gets a noseful of regret. It's nature's way of saying, "Respect my boundaries!"

452. Peering into the pantries of old, the fungus Penicillium was both a bane and a boon. While some strains spoiled food, others gave us the life-saving penicillin antibiotic. An accurate tale of duality in the world of fungi!

453. We step into the bustling streets of 14th-century London, where whispers of the bubonic plague fill the air. Caused by the bacteria Yersinia pestis, this dark shadow wasn't just a London problem; it spread across Europe. But fear not! In our modern world, handy antibiotics stand guard, ensuring this ancient menace stays in the history books!

454. Yum! Do you know what's responsible for experiencing the flavor of all your favorite foods? The tiny tasters that we call taste buds! With around 10,000 tastebuds perched on our tongue, they ensure we savor a spectrum of flavors. Even though they have a fleeting lifespan of about 10 days, new taste buds are always ready for the tasting!

455. Camouflage experts, step aside for the greater short-horned lizard. With its spiky appearance, this creature can not only change the color of its urine to blend in but also tweak its scent to match its surroundings. This ensures it remains hidden from threats in the arid landscapes of North America. A true master of disguise in the desert.

456. Birdsong might be music to our ears, but the greater honeyguide in Africa has a different tune. With its sharp beak and keen eyes, this bird has a symbiotic relationship with humans. When it's in the mood to share a sweet secret, it produces a "guiding spit" to help lead humans to hidden beehives. Once the humans have harvested the honey, this clever bird enjoys any honey and wax leftovers. A sweet partnership indeed!

457. Like the rivers of our body, veins tirelessly carry life's essentials to every nook and cranny of our body, ensuring it is nourished and thriving. Just like a river carries nutrients to distant lands, our veins ensure every cell gets its share of oxygenated blood and nutrients, keeping us vibrant and full of life!

458. Now, grab your torches, adventurers! We're sneaking into the dimly lit corridors of an ancient Egyptian pyramid. Hidden within the wraps of mummies lies a tale of Mycobacterium tuberculosis. This sneaky bacteria that causes a nasty respiratory virus has been mingling with humans for over 4,000 years. Even the mighty pharaohs weren't immune to its presence!

459. Hiding at bustling markets, perched upon the food displays, Escherichia coli (E. coli) is both a friend and foe. While some strains are harmless, others can lead to serious foodborne illnesses. With proper food handling and hygiene, we dance in harmony with these microscopic maestros.

460. Check out the beaver, nature's builder! With its strong teeth and powerful tail, this clever creature is famous for building excellent dams. But did you know it's also a master at marking its home? It uses a special smelly substance called castoreum to tell other animals, 'This is mine!' And guess what? This beaver scent is so unique that it's even used in making perfumes and flavoring foods. Who knew beavers could be so crafty and significantly impact life outside the forest!

461. Shrink rays at the ready! Let's go microscopic now to explore the vast surface of our skin! Did you know you're carrying around tiny buddies all over your skin? That's right. Mites! Especially fond of our faces, these microscopic explorers help ensure that our skin's ecosystem remains harmonious. Fear not; these tiny critters are helpers, not invaders!

462. Eyes, the unparalleled photographers of our body, always capture countless moments. With each blink, which happens around 15 times a minute, they refresh and prepare for the following snapshot, ensuring our life's photo album is rich, vivid, and high definition.

463. Listen up, let's paint our minds with synesthesia! It's a sensory symphony where hearing a sweet melody can paint your world in vibrant colors. Some synesthetes can taste words or see sounds, experiencing the world in a cascade of intertwined senses!

464. Gloves and safety goggles on, future chemists! Let's explore the alchemist's labs of the Renaissance, where the bacterium Clostridium botulinum was a mystery. Producing a potent neurotoxin was a rare but severe threat. Today, with proper food safety guidelines, we've unlocked the secrets to keeping this ancient menace at bay.

465. Phew! Do you ever find yourself dripping with sweat after a hard workout or running around the park? This is thanks to your sweat glands! Imagine our sweat glands are a bustling city with 250,000 factories, all dedicated to producing... you guessed it, sweat! These sweat glands are hard at work, ensuring you remain cool and fabulous, even under the scorching sun or during a workout marathon.

466. Back into the '80s, we go, where the world celebrates a monumental victory! After 3,000 years of smallpox's reign of terror caused by the variola virus, a global vaccination campaign has finally declared smallpox defeated, proving the power of science and collaboration.

467. Travel back in time when travelers shared stories of a monstrous foodborne illness. Salmonella once sparked fear among those eating at inns and eateries. This group of bacteria, lurking in raw eggs and meats, was a common cause of food poisoning! But now, with our modern kitchen hygiene and strict restaurant regulations, cases of food poisoning are rare!

468. Swinging all the way back into the Roaring '20s, where the H1N1 influenza A virus, having infected a third of the world's population, was the talk of the globe. Today, it's one of the strains we guard against with our yearly flu shots. The past meets the present in the world of viruses!

469. Take a journey with me to the ancient libraries of India, where Sanskrit scrolls from the 5th century BCE are carefully preserved. These scrolls, perhaps once etched on palm leaves, describe the watery woes of cholera caused by the bacteria Vibrio cholerae. Cholera is a tricky ailment that can give you tummy turmoil like no other. The ancient scribes told of its symptoms and helped us connect the dots through history. Talk about a message from the past!

470. Dive deep, but don't try this fantastic feat at home! Under the surface, we will find those who practice static apnea! These breath-holding champions can stay submerged for over 11 minutes, a feat that would leave most of us gasping! It's a dance between mind and body, a testament to the human spirit's ability to push beyond limits!

471. While we use fans and ACs, the African elephant, the largest land animal on earth, has a natural cooling system. It sprays water and feces onto its back in the scorching African heat. This mud bath not only cools them down but also protects their skin from biting insects, ensuring they remain the cool kings and queens of the savannah.

472. Next up, we have the kidneys! Every day, your kidneys meticulously filter 180 liters of blood, keeping all those villainous toxins at bay. They always work overtime, ensuring every drop is of the finest quality. Let's give a round of applause to the kidneys for keeping our bodies safe from any impurities. The true villain-busting superhero of the body!

473. Come along, explorers, and we'll explore the chambers of ancient infirmaries. It's in these halls where the bacterium Streptococcus pyogenes was a known adversary. Responsible for the painful strep throat, it was a challenge for healers of old. Today, with modern medicine, we've got excellent tools to battle this age-old foe.

HISTORICAL ODDITIES & ANCIENT WONDERS

474. Can you imagine a job that involves washing clothing with pee? Yuck! In Ancient Rome, these workers were called "fullers," and they were laundry wizards with the ability to turn urine into laundry detergent. Who knew your pee had such cleaning prowess? A splash of ammonia, nature's own stain remover, that's who!

475. Gather 'round for the tale of the Great Sausage Duel of 1865! Two German politicians settled their beef with a mock duel using sausages. It was a flavorful fight that ended with laughter rather than violence! A historic reminder that sometimes laughter really is the best medicine.

476. Into the wilds of Colombia, we go on the trail of the fabled El Dorado. This mythical city of gold has ignited imaginations for centuries. Hidden in dense jungles, could its riches still be waiting?

477. Underground, in the city of Naours, France, stands as a silent witness to the horrors of World War I. Its chambers and tunnels provided refuge to soldiers and civilians alike, shielding them from the rain of danger from above.

478. Quick, grab your goggles! We've landed in Bunol, Spain, for La Tomatina, the world's largest tomato fight. Every year, the town erupts in a tomato-tossing extravaganza, painting the streets red with squishy, squashy fun!

479. Set sail with me to Easter Island, where the Moai statues stand tall. These stone giants, crafted by the Rapa Nui people centuries ago, weigh up to 82 tons each. Their creation and transportation remain a puzzle, as intriguing as the statues themselves.

480. Ready your treasure maps! In 1992, a father and son in Suffolk, England, unearthed the Hoxne Hoard, a spectacular Roman treasure buried in a villa. Coins, jewelry, and spoons worth millions are a glittering glimpse into Roman luxury.

481. Journey to Egypt's Valley of the Kings, where the undiscovered tomb of Ramesses VIII could hold untold riches. This missing piece of pharaonic history awaits its reveal by intrepid archaeologists. What secrets might it hold?

482. Take a deep breath and dive with me into the Atlantic, where the Atocha, a Spanish galleon, sank in 1622. Discovered in 1985, this shipwreck brims with silver bars, gold coins, and emeralds—a sunken fortune from the deep!

483. Next, let's chill out with the "ice cutters" of yesteryears! Before the hum of modern refrigerators, these frosty and frigid fellows harvested massive blocks of ice. These kept food fresh during the hottest of summers. Who needs a fridge when you've got an ice cutter?

484. Shh! We're sneaking into the Taj Mahal's secret chambers. Legends whisper of hidden treasures within this architectural wonder. Could jewels and gold be concealed here? The mystery of the Taj awaits!

485. On your marks for a zany trip to the 1904 St. Louis Olympic marathon. Missing athletes, dust clouds, and dog chases made this race a marathon of mishaps. The race was so haphazard that the first-place finisher had actually traveled part of the way by car, making it one of the most chaotic and controversial races in Olympic history!

486. Fasten your time belts; we're whizzing to 1637 Netherlands during the dazzling days of Tulip Mania! Tulips became so valuable that they were worth more than houses. People trading fortunes for flowers? Now that's what I call floral frenzy!

487. Get your metal detectors buzzing! We're off to Staffordshire, England, where the largest hoard of Anglo-Saxon gold and silver was found in 2009. War gear and religious artifacts worth millions, a shining peek into medieval artistry.

488. Check your fruit baskets for one of these hot commodities of the past! In the opulent era of the 18th century, "pineapple renters" showcased this exotic fruit. Pineapples, a symbol of luxury, were rented out by the hour for display at posh parties, showcasing wealth and worldliness. Imagine not being able to find these fancy fruits at your local grocery store!

489. Ahoy, mateys! The tales of pirates aren't just for storybooks. The Whydah Gally was discovered off Cape Cod in 1984. It was a ship that sailed the high seas under the black flag. The only confirmed pirate shipwreck ever found brought to life tales of treasures and high-sea adventures. Ready to set sail?

490. Travel back to one of history's biggest mysteries: the Lost Colony of Roanoke. Established in 1585 in present-day North Carolina, its settlers vanished without a trace, leaving only the cryptic word CROATOAN carved into a tree. Their fate remains one of the New World's most haunting enigmas.

491. Wading into the world of wellness, behold the "leech collectors." These brave workers ventured into murky marshes and collected leeches by letting them latch onto their legs. Once they had collected enough leeches, they would head off to sell them to doctors and apothecaries. Talk about a job that sucks!

492. Before diving into the Atlantic's depths, let us take a moment to reflect on the tragedy that occurred on April 14, 1912. On that fateful day, the infamous "unsinkable" ship, the Titanic, struck an iceberg. Unfortunately, many lives were lost that day, and the Titanic itself was also thought to be lost that day. However, 73 years after it sank, it was located in the North Atlantic Ocean in 1985. A discovery thought to bring historic comfort and answers to a grieving nation.

493. Next, let's take a look at the job of medieval exterminators! Before the age of modern pest-busters, Victorian "rat catchers" were the rodent wranglers. Armed with traps and a nose for finding rat hideouts, they ensured homes echoed with human laughter, not rodent rumbles. Rats, be warned!

494. Can you imagine an entire world right beneath your feet? Welcome to The Sơn Đoòng Cave in Vietnam, nature's amazing underground wonderland. This colossal cave boasts a river, a lush jungle, and a unique climate. It's a subterranean world where shadows dance and echoes sing!

495. Hold onto your crowns, everyone! In the grand palaces of old, the "groom of the close stool" had a unique royal duty. This trusted aide would assist monarchs during their private restroom moments, ensuring the royal "throne" was always ready and pristine. They'd always set up, clean up, and maintain discretion. A position that's close to the throne!

496. Let's travel to the heart of England, where the Uffington White Horse gallops across the hills! This prehistoric hill figure, shaped like a horse, is over 3,000 years old and stretches 360 feet. Its purpose – a symbol, a landmark, or something else – is as puzzling as its striking form.

497. March into the Scottish Highlands on the hunt for Bonnie Prince Charlie's lost treasure. Lost since the 18th-century Jacobite Rebellion, this treasure could contain historical artifacts from a pivotal moment in Scottish history.

498. Hiking boots on as we explore India's Ellora Caves. These rock-cut temples and monasteries from the 5th to 10th centuries represent various Indian religions. Their artistic and architectural splendor leaves visitors in awe.

499. Saddle up for a wild ride to Arizona's Superstition Mountains. We're tracking down the Lost Dutchman's Gold Mine, a legendary source of gold that has lured treasure hunters for decades. But beware, the mountains keep their secrets!

500. Blast off to 1835, when a New York newspaper claimed creatures were on the moon! Bat people and unicorns, oh my! These fictional reports were written by Richard Adams Locke, a journalist who intended them as satire, but many readers believed the tales.

501. Look up! It's raining cats! In 1960s Borneo, parachuting pussycats descended from the skies to chase away pesky rats. This unconventional method was part of a malaria control program, where the cats were deployed to curb the rat population that burgeoned after disease-carrying mosquitoes were eradicated.

502. Off the coast of Japan, the Yonaguni Monument lies submerged. These underwater formations, discovered in 1986, have sparked debates among experts. Are they natural geological formations or remnants of a lost civilization? The mystery deepens with every dive.

503. Hold your breath and tiptoe into the Edinburgh Vaults, where secrets of the past echo off the walls! Once buzzing with shops, these underground chambers turned into hideouts for mysterious figures. Imagine sneaking around in the dim light, uncovering hidden treasures and ghostly tales from the 18th century. It's like stepping into a secret world under the city streets!

504. Time to travel back to 1954 near Egypt's Great Pyramid of Giza. Archaeologists uncovered the Solar Boat, a full-sized vessel meant for Pharaoh Khufu's afterlife journey. It's an ancient marvel of engineering, preserved for millennia!

505. Pinch those noses again, explorers; this next job is a doozy! When the moon rose above the horizon, "night soil men" would emerge. Before the wonders of modern plumbing, these nocturnal heroes collected human waste from homes. Their moonlit missions kept cities pristine and nights a tad less...fragrant.

506. Standing tall in France, the Carnac stones are a dense collection of over 3,000 prehistoric rocks. Erected between 4500 and 3300 BCE, their purpose – whether religious, astronomical, or something else – remains debatable.

507. Let's climb high into the Andes Mountains of Peru to the hidden city of Machu Picchu. Discovered by Hiram Bingham in 1911, this Incan masterpiece, with its terraced fields and sophisticated stonework, raises questions about its purpose. A royal estate? A sacred retreat? The mountains whisper ancient tales.

508. All aboard for a treasure hunt on Florida's shores! Seek the 1715 Treasure Fleet, sunken in a hurricane and yielding riches since 1961. These Spanish galleons, laden with New World gold and jewels, are a diver's dream!

509. Journey to the heart of Rome, where the Pantheon, built around 125 CE, is a testament to Roman architectural genius. Its dome, the largest unreinforced concrete dome in the world, is an awe-inspiring wonder.

510. Imagine a job making crafts using...urine. In the aromatic world of leather, "tanners" toiled tirelessly. They transformed raw hides into durable leather utilizing water, urine, and tannin-rich
potions. Crafting the very fabric of everyday life, from belts to book bindings. Think about that next time you appreciate our modern-day leather!

511. Pinch your noses; we're off to 1858 London, where the River Thames was stinkier than a pile of dirty socks! The Great Stink eventually led to the creation of London's modern sewer system, designed by engineer Joseph Bazalgette, which vastly improved the city's sanitation and health.

512. Trek through Sri Lanka's lush jungles in search of the Golden Cave Temple. Said to hold a room filled with golden statues and gems, this temple is a hidden gem in the heart of the jungle, awaiting discovery.

513. Set sail on a Caribbean adventure, following the treasure map of pirate Captain Kidd. Said to be buried on a remote island, this legendary pirate's loot has eluded seekers for centuries. Gold and jewels under the tropical sun?

514. Detector wands at the ready! Journey to Viking-era York, England, where a father and son duo found the Vale of York Hoard. Viking silver, coins, and treasures, a shining slice of history under our feet!

515. Lace up your hiking boots for an Andean adventure! We're searching for Peru's Llanganates Treasure, rumored to be hidden in Inca gold. This legendary trove, evading Spanish conquistadors, still calls to treasure hunters today.

516. Stroll through a Kansas cornfield where the steamboat Arabia, sunk in 1856, was found in 1988. Packed with 19th-century goods, it's a submerged treasure trove of everyday items, a peek into life from a bygone era.

517. Dive masks on, deep-sea explorers! We're plunging into the waters near Colombia to find the sunken San José galleon. Lost in 1708, it's a treasure chest of gold, silver, and emeralds resting on the ocean floor, just waiting for discovery!

518. We're waddling over to 1958 London, where a penguin's great escape from the zoo amused the city! This clever bird, named Juanita, waddled her way to freedom, taking a tour around London before she was safely returned to the zoo.

519. Can you imagine a room filled with shimmering gold and amber? The Amber Room was just that! Adorned with amber panels and gold, it was a sight to behold. But during World War II, the Nazis had their eyes on it. They looted this masterpiece; since then, its location has become one of the war's most captivating mysteries. Will it ever be found?

520. Sneak through the secret tunnels of Orvieto, the city that hides around 1,200 tunnels and caves! Where every turn could lead to a hidden treasure or an ancient artifact. Exploring these tunnels is like uncovering the mysteries of a city built on secrets!

521. Zoom to 1857, when a tailless comet sighting sent the world into a frenzy! People feared it would crash into earth, causing worldwide panic. But, spoiler alert, the earth is still here, and the comet harmlessly passed by!

522. Ahead, we'll encounter a job with a really tricky name! Dive deep into the world of "honey dippers!" While this job may sound sweet, it's actually quite icky! Before we had fancy plumbing, these hardy folks tackled privies and cesspits, removing human poop with just a long pole and a scoop. Talk about diving into a sticky...or stinky situation!

523. Dive deep underground into the mysterious city of Derinkuyu. It's a hidden world 200 feet below the surface! Picture sneaking through secret passages, discovering hidden rooms, and unraveling the mysteries of the people who lived here long ago. It's like being a detective in a subterranean wonderland!

524. Deep into flickering factories, "matchstick girls" would meticulously craft tiny sticks that would burst into flame. Unbeknownst to them, the white phosphorus they used to make them was very harmful. The effects on their health caused suffering and sparked the beginnings of early labor rights movements. A sad tale with a monumental mark on history!

525. Next, let's head to the arid plains of Peru, where the Nazca Lines etch tales into the earth. Large enough to be fully seen only from the air, these mysterious geoglyphs depict various figures and shapes. Created by the Nazca culture over 2,000 years ago, their purpose – whether astronomical, ritualistic, or artistic – is still a mystery.

526. Up, up, we climb! Scaling the skies, "flagpole painters" brushed against the clouds. Braving dizzying heights and unpredictable weather, they meticulously applied layers upon layers of protective paint. Their high-flying feats ensured flagpoles everywhere gleamed with pride, standing tall and rust-free for all to see. Proud patriots of the past!

527. Climb through the ancient cave city of Uplistsikhe, where every cave and tunnel has a story to tell. Living in these rock-carved homes, you could be a brave warrior or a wise sage. It's like wandering through a giant stone community full of history and mystery!

528. Deep in the jungles of Guatemala, a secret lay buried for centuries. The ancient Mayan city of El Mirador was a testament to a civilization's grandeur. When it was rediscovered in 1926, the world was introduced to the largest pyramid by volume. A silent sentinel, it showcased the architectural prowess of the Mayans. What other secrets do these jungles hold?

529. Imagine a hidden treasure in the Cambodian jungles – that's Angkor Wat! This sprawling temple complex, the largest religious monument in the world, is a maze of wonders. Its walls are adorned with intricate carvings depicting ancient myths and history, inviting us to unravel its stories.

530. Hold onto your hats, young explorers! We're zooming to 1932 Australia, where emus and soldiers faced off in a feathery frenzy! The emus were on a crop-crunching spree, and the military thought they'd outsmart them. The army struggled to control the emu population, proving how tricky and resilient these large birds can be!

531. Explore one of the 7 wonders of the world, the city of Petra in Jordan. The city is entirely carved from rose-red cliffs and is an architectural marvel. Beyond its iconic façades, the city showcases an advanced water conduit system. Although parts of this ancient city have been unearthed, approximately 85 percent is still buried. An unearthed testament to the ingenuity of its ancient inhabitants.

532. Embark on a polar quest to find Ernest Shackleton's lost ship, Endurance, beneath Antarctica's ice. Lost in 1915, uncovering it would reveal secrets of one of history's most daring explorations. A frozen treasure under the ice!

533. Climb to hidden peaks in Cambodia, where a secret has been held for ages! The lost city of Mahendraparvata of the Khmer Empire was a riddle waiting to be solved. In 2012, using laser technology, its ruins were unveiled after being buried beneath the intricate foliage of the forest. A city that once bustled with life now reveals tales of its past!

534. Strap on your hiking boots! We're scaling the cliffs near the Dead Sea, where in 1947, young Bedouin shepherds discovered the ancient Dead Sea Scrolls in hidden caves. These scrolls are a priceless window into the past!

535. Meet folks with a nose for what goes! In the quest for freshness, "odor judges" took a deep breath for science. Tasked with sniffing out the effectiveness of hygiene products, their keen noses played a pivotal role in developing deodorants, ensuring the world smelled just a tad bit better. Our noses appreciate their sacrifice!

536. Up, up, and away to 1846 New York, where a fire balloon caused a citywide panic! This hot air balloon, carrying a fire-powered lantern, drifted over the city, leading many to believe it was a flaming U.F.O. or a comet about to crash!

537. Let's venture to Namibia's Skeleton Coast, where the Bom Jesus, a lost Portuguese ship, was found. Over 500 years old and packed with gold coins, it's a sandy treasure trove hidden among haunting shipwrecks.

538. The next stop is Strasbourg, 1518, where the streets turned into a non-stop dance party! People boogied without a break for days, caught in a mysterious dancing fever. This puzzling event affected around 400 people; some even danced to their exhaustion, making it one of history's most bizarre medical mysteries.

539. Excavation equipment ready, adventurers? Let's dig with British archaeologist Sir Austen Henry Layard to find the Assyrian capital, Nimrud. Thanks to Layard, it was brought back to light in the mid-19th century. His excavations unveiled the city's grandeur, including statues, reliefs, and the iconic winged lamassu. Layard's discoveries showcased the splendor of the Assyrian Empire to the world.

540. Scuba dive down, down, down! Shipwrecked off the coast of Columbia, San José Galleon held treasures that many dreamt of finding. Sunk by the British over 300 years ago, it was finally found off the coast of Colombia in 2015. This discovery has since sparked many debates over who has the rightful claim to its sunken fortune. A watery treasure chest of riches!

541. Step into the golden history of India at the Padmanabhaswamy Temple. In 2011, secret vaults revealed a treasure trove of gold and jewels. This discovery showcases the incredible wealth and history hidden in ancient temples.

542. Grab your nose plugs again! Treading the cobbled streets, "pure finders" turned canine contributions into tanning treasures. Dog droppings, rich in enzymes that would help to turn leather hides soft and supple, were an in-demand ingredient in the leather tanning process. Imagine knowing your satchel contained a pooch poop surprise!

543. Dive in and enjoy our next whale of a tale! "Whale blubber processors" turned the fatty layers of these marine giants into precious oil. This golden elixir lit homes across the world long before electric bulbs. Now that's a HUGE job to fulfill!

544. Zoom back thousands of years to Matera, Italy, where the "Sassi" cave dwellings are like a time machine! These ancient homes, carved into cliffs, are like exploring a giant, rocky maze. Imagine living in these caves, cooking over stone fireplaces, and playing in the moonlit shadows. It's like being part of a historical movie set, but it's all real!

545. Let's sail to the 1700s, where squabbling over a sailor's ear sparked a real maritime match! After a British captain claimed a Spanish coast guard cut off his ear, Britain declared war on Spain, leading to a more significant conflict known as the War of Jenkins' Ear.

546. Grab your flashlights, explorers; we are going down beneath the ground to explore some incredible underground locations! First, let's travel beneath Turkey's ancient landscape, where the Derinkuyu underground city unveils layers of history. This sprawling subterranean city is equipped with intricate ventilation shafts and stables. Peculiar as it may seem, it once sheltered up to 20,000 inhabitants from threats above!

547. Ships ahoy! On the swaying decks of naval ships, "loblolly boys" were the unsung heroes of the high seas. Amidst cannon fire and rolling waves, they fetched water, held instruments, and even assisted during surgeries. Ensuring sailors sailed smoothly through both storms and sickness. The seasick surgeons of the past!

548. All aboard for the Scottish Orkney Islands! The village of Skara Brae, unearthed in 1850, offers a window into life over 5,000 years ago. Its well-preserved stone structures provide rare insights into Neolithic living.

549. Fancy a treasure hunt? Let's dive into the smelly sewers with the "toshers" of Victorian London. These daring adventurers scavenged the city's sewage systems for hidden gems, proving that amidst the muck, one person's trash is another's treasure. Pirates, take notes!

550. Unravel the secrets of the Longyou Caves in China, a mysterious place filled with water and wonder. These hand-carved caves are like a puzzle waiting to be solved. Imagine being the first to discover them, diving into the unknown, and making an epic discovery!

551. Journeying to the rose-red cliffs of Jordan, the city of Petra beckons. With structures like Al-Khazneh carved directly into the rock, this ancient city, likely established as early as 312 BCE, blends architectural genius and mystery. Its purpose, whether as a temple or a royal tomb, adds to its allure.

552. Back aboard our scientific submarine! Defending down to visit the coast of South Carolina, where a shipwreck with a golden secret lay hidden. The S.S. Central America sank over 130 years earlier and was discovered in 1988. Laden with gold; it was a treasure hunter's dream come true!

553. Grab your hiking boots for a trek to Bolivia's Tiwanaku. This pre-Incan city, flourishing from 300 to 1000 CE, showcases precise stonework and iconic structures like the Gateway of the Sun, hinting at a sophisticated and enigmatic civilization.

554. Imagine an underground world made of salt? Imagine no more; welcome to the Wieliczka Salt Mine in Poland. This architectural feat is a testament to human artistry and Endurance. Mined since the 13th century, its depths reveal chapels, sculptures, and chandeliers, all meticulously carved from salt, shimmering in the dim underground light.

555. Up next is a finding of great debate! In Greece, Helike was located in 2001, having been submerged for over 2,000 years! Experts have debated if this Greek city is the "real" Atlantis. An ancient town that nature had claimed, now revealed to the world!

556. Head to the Rocky Mountains where, in 2010, art dealer Forrest Fenn claimed to have hidden a chest full of gold, jewels, and other valuables. This modern treasure hunt captivates adventurers with its promise of riches and mystery.

557. Let's venture to the Yucatán Peninsula. Here, the ancient Mayan city of Chichen Itza stands proud. Its iconic pyramid, El Castillo, aligns perfectly with the equinoxes, showcasing the Mayans' advanced understanding of astronomy and their architectural prowess.

558. Get ready for a meaty mystery in 1876 Kentucky, where meat fell from the sky! This bizarre, meaty meteorological event left everyone scratching their heads, with some theorizing the meat was regurgitated by vultures flying overhead.

559. Turn on those taste buds as we explore a job as sweet as they come! Behind gleaming counters, "soda jerks" were the maestros of sweet delights. They mixed syrups and seltzer with a flourish, crafting delightful drinks and ice cream sundaes, turning each visit into a sugary spectacle. Talk about a tasty talent!

560. Ahoy, Archeological adventurers! Let's explore the ancient city of Troy, long thought to be a myth from Homer's epics. Troy was rediscovered in the late 19th century by archaeologist Heinrich Schliemann in modern-day Turkey. A plethora of history is finally located!

561. Be amazed by the history found in the city of Xi'an, China. Here, a group of farmers hoped to find water but stumbled upon something more astonishing. In 1974, they unearthed the Terracotta Army, thousands of life-sized clay soldiers, each with unique features. An emperor's afterlife guard, frozen in time!

562. Let's slither over to learn about a job that will give you a shiver! Snake milkers would gently squeeze venom from snake fangs! And guess what? This venom is still used for medical tests, life-saving medicines, and antivenoms to help treat snake bites! A courageous career indeed!

563. Whisper legends with the locals tell of the "White City" hidden deep within the Honduran rainforests. For years, many thought it was just a myth. But in 2012, using advanced LiDAR technology, the existence of La Ciudad Blanca was confirmed. A city lost in time, waiting to share its stories.

564. Fasten your nose plugs as we journey to Medieval England, where "gong farmers" were the unsung heroes of cleanliness. Delving deep into cesspits and privies, or toilets, they ensured that the streets remained spick and span by disposing of human waste. Talk about a dirty job!

565. Explore the Longyou Caves in China, a marvel of ancient engineering. Discovered in 1992, these hand-carved caves, with no historical records of their creation, are a focal point of intrigue and wonder.

566. Join me as we journey to the English countryside, where Stonehenge stands tall. This prehistoric circle of massive stones, some transported over 150 miles, has been a beacon of mystery for nearly 5,000 years. Was it an ancient temple or a cosmic calendar? The stones silently guard their secrets.

567. Travel to the heart of Mexico to explore Teotihuacan. This ancient city, with its majestic Pyramids of the Sun and Moon, dates back to the first century B.C.E. Its original builders remain unknown, adding an air of mystery to its grandeur.

568. Imagine trying to read a book in a different language with no way to translate it? This is how historians felt, but thanks to The Rosetta Stone, critical to deciphering Egyptian hieroglyphs. They were finally able to understand these masterpieces of communication! A French soldier stumbled upon the Rosetta Stone during Napoleon's Egyptian campaign in 1799, a significant find for the future!

569. Don't look down; we're heading up rather high! Perched high in towers, "fire lookouts" surveyed vast forests. With keen eyes and essential tools, they detected the earliest signs of smoke in the trees. Their alerts were pivotal in early wildfire response, making them the silent sentinels of the forest. Regular smoke alarms of the past!

570. Treasure hunting is not just something you see in the movies! Hidden away in Afghanistan was the Bactrian Gold, a collection of over 20,000 gold ornaments. Rediscovered in 2003 after being safeguarded from looters, it showcased the rich history and craftsmanship of the region.

571. Dig down with archeologists in 1974, when China unveiled an army frozen in time. The Terracotta Army, with over 8,000 life-sized figures, stands guard, a silent entourage built for the first Emperor of China.

572. Come with me and explore the plains of Wiltshire, England, where the Avebury stone circle is even larger and older than Stonehenge. This feat stands as a silent guardian of the past. But here's a twist: Its purpose, whether ceremonial or astronomical, is a riddle from prehistory. However, its presence is a powerful reminder of ancient peoples.

573. Dive suits on! Join us in exploring the world's oldest known shipwreck in the Black Sea. Dating back to 400 B.C., this ancient Greek vessel holds past secrets deep under the waves. A sunken time capsule is calling!

574. Flash! 1859's skies lit up with the most magnificent solar storm, the Carrington Event, zapping telegraphs and dazzling the world. The Carrington Event, named after astronomer Richard Carrington, was the first recognized instance of a solar flare affecting earth's magnetosphere and remains one of the most significant geomagnetic events on record.

575. Adventure to a city long forgotten by the world. Although locals remembered its existence, the world called it "The Lost City of the Incas." Thanks to the explorations of Hiram Bingham, the ruins of Machu Picchu were introduced to the world in 1911. An abandoned city with many tales to tell!

576. Grab your shovels; we're off to Oak Island, Nova Scotia, to unearth the secrets of the Money Pit. For over 200 years, this spot has tantalized treasure hunters with tales of buried pirate gold. What lies beneath, we wonder?

577. Wow! Look around, explorers, what an incredible site! Nature puts on a celestial show in New Zealand's Waitomo Glowworm Caves. Thousands of glowworms light up the darkness, creating a mesmerizing subterranean galaxy. An underground wonder inhabited by a spectacularly illuminating insect!

578. Oops! In 1788, an army fought...itself! A mix-up turned into a mash-up, with soldiers on the same side battling each other. This self-inflicted skirmish, known as the Battle of Karánsebes, reportedly occurred during the Austro-Turkish War when different corps of the Habsburg army mistook each other for the enemy.

579. Get ready to explore the eight-level fortress of Kaymaklı! Each level is a new adventure, with stables, cellars, and ancient chapels. It's like exploring a castle but underground. You could be a knight on a quest or a princess uncovering ancient secrets!

580. Now, let's cool off in the dugouts of Coober Pedy, Australia's underground gem! Imagine living in a house carved into the earth, where sparkling opals might be found under your bed. It's like being part of a secret, underground community where every day is a treasure hunt!

581. Climb to the top of Shibaozhai's wooden pagoda, built against a towering cliff. Imagine being a fearless adventurer, scaling the heights to uncover ancient legends and breathtaking views. It's like conquering a castle in the sky!

582. A war over... pastries? In 1838, Mexico and France had a flaky feud over a looted bakery. The Pastry War, sparked by damages claimed by a French pastry chef, escalated into a military conflict involving naval blockades, eventually leading to a settlement where Mexico agreed to pay the claimed damages.

583. Waddle to Phillip Island, Australia, for the cutest parade ever! Every evening, little penguins strut from the sea to their burrows in a delightful waddle. This unique natural event has become a significant tourist attraction, bringing thousands to witness the adorable march of these tiny penguins.

584. Far beneath the icy waters of the Canadian Arctic lay the H.M.S. Erebus. Part of Sir John Franklin's lost Arctic expedition, its whereabouts remained a mystery until 2014. When finally found, it offered clues to a chilling tale of exploration and a strive to survive.

585. Imagine wild animals running loose in New York City! In 1874, a newspaper falsely reported animals had escaped from Central Park Zoo, causing a citywide uproar. It turned out to be a big hoax, but it was a wild tale!

586. Splash into the Basilica Cistern in Istanbul, a hidden water world supported by majestic marble columns. Picture yourself as an explorer discovering an ancient city's secret water supply. It's like finding a lost kingdom hidden beneath the bustling streets!

587. Dive deep into the waters, and you might find treasures from the past! The Antikythera Mechanism, an ancient Greek device retrieved from a shipwreck in 1901, was a marvel. An analog computer from bygone times, its intricate design left the world in awe. A testament to the genius of ancient inventors!

588. Let's unravel the Berners Street Hoax of 1810, a day of utter chaos! A mischievous prankster, Theodore Hook bet he could turn any house into London's most famous address. He sent hundreds of visitors, from bakers to dignitaries, to one unsuspecting home, creating a day of mayhem and amusement.

589. Tales of the city of Ubar were mentioned in many ancient texts. But where was it? In the 1990s, researchers pinpointed its location in the Rub' al Khali desert of Oman using modern satellite imagery. A city once lost in the sands of time is now found with the help of the stars!

590. Torches in hand, we're tiptoeing into Egypt's Valley of the Kings. Here, Howard Carter stumbled upon Pharaoh Tutankhamun's tomb in 1922, a hidden chamber of golden treasures that whispers tales of ancient Egyptian grandeur.

591. Marvel at the Great Pyramid of Giza! Towering over the Egyptian sands, this ancient wonder, the oldest of the Seven Wonders of the Ancient World, has intrigued scholars for centuries. Built over 4,500 years ago, it's a marvel of engineering, with its precise alignment and massive limestone blocks. How it was constructed remains a captivating mystery!

592. Imagine finding a treasure trove of knowledge in an old manuscript! The Palimpsest of Archimedes, discovered in 1906, was just that. This 10th-century manuscript revealed unknown works of the ancient mathematician. It's a reminder that history always has more stories to share; sometimes, they're written between the lines.

593. Marvel at Ohio's Serpent Mound, a prehistoric effigy mound shaped like a winding snake. Believed to be built by the Adena culture around 1000 BCE, its purpose, whether astronomical, ritualistic, or symbolic, is a topic of endless debate.

594. Let's trudge through the muck to meet the Mud-caked "mudlarks" who scoured riverbanks for hidden treasures. Working hard, especially along the Thames River, these persistent scavengers would unearth everything from lost coins to forgotten trinkets. Proving that sometimes, dirt does indeed dazzle!

595. Whoosh! We're off to 1919 Boston, where a sticky wave of molasses swept through the streets! A giant storage tank burst, unleashing a sugary tsunami. This disaster caused many problems for the people of Boston and ultimately led to stricter regulations on industrial storage tanks.

596. Flippers on, deep sea divers! Time to explore a city once thought to be only a legend. In this case, this legend holds a hint of truth. Off the coast of India, the city of Dwarka was found submerged. In the 1980s, this discovery bridged the gap between mythology and history. Exposing a town where legends once walked!

597. Put away your flashlights because we are headed into the night to meet a group of human lampposts! As dusk draped the city, "lamplighters" worked tirelessly to cast a warm glow on cobblestone streets. With long poles and a touch of unique skill, they lit and maintained gas lamps. Their nightly ritual transformed shadowy lanes into shimmering pathways, guiding the way for all nocturnal wanderers.

598. Look up, and you'll see China's Leshan Giant Buddha, the largest stone Buddha in the world. Carved in the 8th century, this colossal statue is a testament to devotion and ancient Chinese artistry.

599. Let's slide into the world of "snail farmers," an unusual job from the past. These farmers spent their days raising snails, not as pets, but for food and sometimes medicine. It was a job that required patience and a unique interest in these slow, slimy creatures. Snail farming: a curious and slimy profession from history!

600. Shimmy up the rooftops with the "chimney sweeps." These sooty daredevils braved the dark, narrow flues, sliding down each one to clear them out and ensure that homes remained cozy and smoke-free. A dance with danger, but all in a day's work for these chimney champions!

601. Flying from India to Turkey, we find Göbekli Tepe, the world's oldest known temple. Dating back to the 10th millennium B.C.E., this site predates Stonehenge by over 6,000 years. Its purpose, whether spiritual or communal, remains one of archaeology's greatest enigmas.

602. Buckle up! In 1982, Larry Walters, a man with a dream and 45 helium balloons, soared into the sky in a lawn chair! Floating over Los Angeles, he reached 16,000 feet before safely landing. A sky-high adventure on a simple chair, proving that sometimes, the sky's the limit!

603. Join the search for the lost Fabergé Eggs, Russian imperial treasures of unmatched craftsmanship. Jeweler Carl Fabergé created these missing masterpieces among the world's most sought-after artifacts. Where could they be?

604. Breaking news, adventurers: our next job is quite the story! Amidst the clanging of clattering keys, "linotype operators" crafted the news. These skilled artisans set type for newspapers, ensuring big and small stories reached eager readers with their morning tea. A career that's hot off the press!

605. Deep in the Judean Desert, a treasure was waiting. The Dead Sea Scrolls, ancient Jewish texts, were hidden in the Qumran Caves. In 1947, a curious Bedouin shepherd stumbled upon these scrolls, revealing a glimpse into early Jewish religious practices and beliefs!

606. Read the secrets of the Vinland Map, unveiled in the 1960s; it was believed to be the first map depicting part of America. Its authenticity sparked debates, but its discovery challenged our understanding of history.

607. Walk the fantastic stone paths of Sacsayhuamán in Peru. This fortress, a testament to Incan architectural skill, features stones weighing over 100 tons. Constructed in the 15th century without modern tools, it is a puzzle of historical engineering.

608. Our next tale is quite the tragic one! Donning beaked masks filled with herbs, "plague doctors" would brave the streets during the darkest times. Their iconic outfits weren't just for show; they were some of the earliest attempts at protective gear against germs and disease. Mysterious medics with peculiar methods!

609. Let's continue our exploration, where we'll discover one of the biggest mysteries of all! The Bermuda Triangle, a place overflowing with mysteries, tells tales of vanished ships. The S.S. Cotopaxi was one such ship that disappeared in 1925. For 95 years, its fate remained a riddle. But in 2020, off Florida's coast, the ship was found. A maritime enigma, finally solved!

610. Next, we make our way to the underground fortress of Nushabad, believed to have been built about 1,500 years ago! Where secret traps and hidden passages were made to guard this ancient treasure. Exploring this fortress is like being part of a thrilling adventure story, where mysteries await everywhere!

ADAPTATIONS & ABILITIES: NATURE'S SUPERPOWERS

611. Let's soar to the skies of South America, where the Andean condor rules the air. With a wingspan reaching up to 10 feet, this bird can glide for hours without flapping its wings. This incredible ability is due to thermal air currents and its massive wing area, making it a master of energy-efficient travel in the sky.

612. Get ready for a high-flying adventure with the bar-tailed godwit! Skimming over coastal mudflats, this bird's super-sensitive bill is like a built-in weather station. It can feel the slightest changes in air pressure, tipping off our feathered friend about incoming storms. This helps it make intelligent, timely decisions during its epic migrations. A bird with a barometer for a beak!

613. Beware the ocean's crafty hunter, the hammerhead shark! With its uniquely shaped head, it's not just a bizarre sight—it's a panoramic vision powerhouse! Gliding through tropical seas, this shark's odd design isn't just for show. It expands its visual range and supercharges its ability to detect the electric pulses of unseen prey. A peculiar look that packs a powerful predatory punch!

614. Journey to the bustling markets of Africa, where the Medfly began its global escapade. These tiny invaders have now spread their wings to North and South America, Europe, and Asia, leaving a trail of damaged fruits and veggies. A pint-sized insect with an enormous appetite!

615. Stay out of these waters, adventurers! In the swamps, the American alligator feels the subtlest ripples in the water. Specialized organs on its snout help detect these vibrations, revealing a fish's dart or a bird's splash. A lurking danger with an exceptional radar!

616. Next, we explore the stickiest tale of all time! Imagine a ship from the Black and Caspian seas docking in North America. But hidden in its ballast water are the zebra mussels. These invasive and uninvited guests quickly made themselves at home, causing a ruckus in waterways and outcompeting the locals. A problem still plaguing waterways today!

617. Buzzing through sun-dappled meadows, honeybees dance and navigate, guided by the sun's rays. Even when clouds hide the sun, polarized light patterns help to guide them, ensuring they always find their way back to the hive. A beautiful display of nature's natural radar!

618. Is it a fish or a snake? Wow! American lakes have a new predator: the northern snakehead fish from Asia. They're on the hunt for prey and outcompeting local fish. This is turning the aquatic balance on its head. A master of trickery from below the waves!

619. Into the caves of Europe, we go! The olm, a blind salamander, navigates the dark with heightened senses. Without eyes, it relies on touch, taste, and hearing to find its way. It's a master of echolocation, bouncing sound waves off its surroundings to paint a picture of its world. Talk about a superpowered salamander!

620. Grab your snow shovels and dig through a winter wonderland with the reindeer! Reindeer use their sturdy antlers to dig through the deep snow and uncover edible foliage hidden beneath. You might think only the male deer are gifted with this cunning adaptation, but reindeer are the only deer species where both boys and girls can grow antlers! A frosty twist on this festive fact!

621. All aboard the submarine for a sinking expedition! Deep in the Atlantic's coral reefs, the lionfish, a venomous newcomer from the Indo-Pacific region, is causing quite a stir. They live a high life with no natural predators, dining on native fish and causing underwater chaos. Accurately named, this underwater invader aims to become king of the underwater pride!

622. Zooming through the sky, meet the peregrine falcon, the fastest flyer in the bird world! When diving after their prey, these amazing birds can reach speeds over 240 miles per hour, making them the fastest animals on Earth. That's even speedier than a race car! They use this super speed to catch other birds right out of the air. With their sharp eyes and quick wings, peregrine falcons are like the superheroes of the sky!

623. Gather round adventurers, and let me tell you a tale of a species attempting to take over the world, Australia's cane toad. Originally from Central and South America, cane toads were introduced to combat beetles harming sugar cane crops. But, in a plot twist, they turned from the heroes to the villains, threatening native wildlife with their toxic antics and rapid reproduction. A hopping tale with a twist!

624. Bustling Asian ports are the starting point for the Asian long-horned beetle's journey. This stowaway has taken its maiden voyage to faraway lands and is now drilling into hardwood trees in North America and Europe! This tiny horned foe is leaving a trail of destruction in its wake!

625. Phew! Hold your noses, smell specialists. The brown marmorated stink bug, an East Asian native, is now seeking shelter in American suburbs. These uninvited guests are causing a stir, munching on crops and sneaking into homes. Talk about a smelly situation!

626. Stop and smell the roses, observationalists! Take a sniff, and you may find our next invader: the European earwig. While they munch on pests like aphids, they're also causing a ruckus in North American gardens, damaging crops and plants.

627. Grab your magnifying glasses; our next species is tiny but mighty! South American forests are home to the Argentine ant, but these tiny invaders have set their sights on global domination. Marching into new territories, they're outcompeting the locals and feasting on crops. These little guys put the A-N-T in tyrant!

628. Lurking in the ocean's depths, the octopus feels and tastes its world. Each sucker, poised on the ends of its tentacles, is a sensor that allows the octopus to sample the flavors of the sea. These sensational sucker sensors also help it distinguish friend from foe. A seemingly simple tool with a hidden purpose!

629. Surfs up, student scientists! It's time to catch a swell and surf to our next invasive insect. In Southern California, palm trees are threatened by the South American palm weevil. These uninvited guests are causing palms to wither and die, ruining the environment, economy, and beautiful views!

630. Get your imaginary infrared goggles ready! In the forest's dappled sunlight, the jewel beetle is on a secret mission. Its shiny armor isn't just for show — it's equipped with built-in infrared sensors! These tiny thermal detectives help the beetle find the coziest spots for its eggs. A dazzling bug with a heat-seeking superpower!

631. Careful in the water! Our next creature is sure to be looking for its next meal! In the vast oceans, sharks patrol with unparalleled olfactory prowess. A single drop of blood, diluted to almost invisibility, can beckon them from miles away, guiding them through the watery abyss to their next meal. A sense fit for a scary movie!

632. Grab your kayaks! North American lakes are being overrun by the curly-leaf pondweed from Eurasia. This aquatic invader is thought to have been released in the 1800s by aquarium hobbyists who were unaware of the environmental impact. It's proliferating, overshadowing native plants and killing off native species. A testimony to why we should never release non-native plants or animals into the wild!

633. Dive with me into the ocean's depths, where the anglerfish lures its prey with a glowing bait! This deep-sea dweller has a bioluminescent lure right above its mouth, attracting curious fish right into its jaws. A deep-sea deception at its finest!

634. Let's float by the water hyacinth, a South American native which floats gracefully in ponds worldwide. But don't be fooled by its beauty because it's plotting a takeover, choking out other plants, and stealing their nutrients. That's a water predator with the plan!

635. Grab your sun hat! On the vast African savannah, elephants are the masters of touch with their incredible trunks. These muscular wonders, boasting over 40,000 muscles, are so precise they can gently pluck a single blade of grass or detect far-off thunderstorms through the ground's subtle tremors. Talk about a sensational snout!

636. Hello! Hello! Echo! Do you hear that, explorers? It sounded like an echo! Resting in the rainforest canopy, the lyrebird sings, its voice echoing with a myriad of sounds. From the songs of other birds to the buzz of chainsaws, its vocal range is a testament to its adaptability and memory. A bird with a unique gift of mimicry!

637. Take a look around! North American landscapes are being transformed by the Russian olive, a tree from Europe and Asia. Its dense growth is overshadowing native vegetation and altering ecosystems. These tactical trees can quickly overtake a backyard or field if allowed to flower! It's wise to nip these trees in the bud before they create a huge problem!

638. Flap your wings, explorers, and soar! As twilight descends, bats take to the skies, not with sight, but with sound. Their high-pitched echolocation paints a sonic picture of the world, pinpointing fluttering moths and navigating the night's maze. Nature's nocturnal radar!

639. Snorkels on, explorers! Let's swim along and explore our next creature's freshwater habitat. Meet the electric catfish! This cunning creature is surrounded by a cloak of electric fields. These fields, invisible to most, light up their world, revealing prey, obstacles, and even potential mates. Nature's most illuminating talent!

640. Hopping across the leafy parks of the United Kingdom and Italy, the gray squirrel, a North American native, is causing a stir. These bushy-tailed newcomers are spreading a deadly virus and claiming the best tree branches, causing many issues for the native red squirrel. A rodent with a ruling plan!

641. Look up! Scaling the walls and ceilings, the gecko shows off its gravity-defying feats. These lizards can strut their stuff on even the slickest surfaces thanks to millions of tiny foot hairs. It's like watching a superhero in action!

642. Scaling the steep cliffs of the European Alps, meet the ibex. These agile climbers have unique hooves: soft, grippy pads for a firm hold and hard edges for precision. It's nature's version of climbing shoes! They can balance on two-inch ledges, defying gravity to stay out of predators' reach. The ibex is nature's own mountain acrobat!

643. Gear up for a garden invasion with the Japanese Knotweed! This pushy plant, originally from East Asia, is causing quite a stir in English gardens. With its super-fast growth, it's not just pushing through pavements but also elbowing out other plants.! This invader is a real-life example of nature's power to take over when it lands in new territories. Talk about a knot-y situation!

644. Next, let's meet a cute critter known for using the landscape to create its own natural refrigerator! The cunning American red squirrel hides its store of food in the snowy forests. Then, it uses its hyper-sensitive nose to sniff out its hidden treasures. Even under layers of snow, its keen nose can locate the caches of food it buried months before!

645. Brace for a dusty adventure on the steppes with the saiga antelope! While we might reach for masks in the swirling dust, these antelopes are perfectly equipped. Their unique noses are nature's dust filters, sifting out the grit and cooling the air. Thanks to their built-in breathing marvels, their breath is as fresh as a breeze!

646. Let's jet off and see our next cunning creature! Soaring high above the Pacific, the bar-tailed godwit is on a marathon flight. This bird covers thousands of miles without a single break! These birds are the ultimate endurance athletes, fueling up on food and burning it off on their epic migrations. A bird with an endless battery!

647. Look up! Pigeons and other birds glide through the skies with a secret guide: Earth's magnetic field. They have an inbuilt GPS, using the planet's invisible forces to navigate, whether winging over bustling cityscapes or weaving through forest canopies. A genuinely remarkable natural navigation system!

648. Let's grab our sun hats and take a trip down south. It looks like Florida's wetlands have a new tourist: the Nile monitor from Africa. These giant lizards, likely released from captivity, are feasting on local wildlife, making it hard for native reptiles to fit in. That's a regular pet-turned-pest if you ask me!

649. Next, let's hop into our submarine and explore the coral reefs, where the pygmy seahorse is the hide-and-seek master. Capable of changing colors and forming superficial bumps called tubercles, this seahorse can render itself nearly invisible by perfectly camouflaging to the textured coral it inhabits. A dime-sized creature with an adaptation big enough to fool any foe!

650. Jump into the freshwater ponds of the USA, where they welcomed the Asian carp with open arms in the 1970s, hoping they'd tackle aquatic weeds. But these fish loved their new job a bit too much, hogging all the plankton and pushing out the local fish. Talk about overstaying their welcome!

651. Can you imagine an insect, smaller than a US dime, causing massive damage to giant trees? This is indeed the case for forests across North America due to the European spruce bark beetle. These bark-boring pests are causing trees to wither and landscapes to transform. A tricky tyrant causing massive economic loss for tree farmers in the United States and Canada.

652. Traveling back in time, we'll explore the transport of our next tiny traveler! Post-World War II, America saw the arrival of the Formosan subterranean termite from East Asia. For over 75 years, these wood-munching invaders have been dining on American homes, causing billions in damages!

653. Let's splash into the underwater world where lobsters are the ultimate taste-testers of the sea! These savvy crustaceans don't just walk on the ocean floor—they're busy tasting it with every step. Their legs and mouthparts are decked out with special sensory hairs, turning each scuttle into a flavor-filled adventure. It's like having a built-in GPS for finding the tastiest treats in the ocean. Now, that's a crustacean with a culinary compass!

654. Gliding through freshwater streams, fish like the rainbow trout feel the currents around them. Their lateral line system, a series of sensors, paints a picture of their watery world, revealing both prey and predator. A showcase of the unique ability of this scaled navigator!

655. Desert detectives, assemble! The spiny-tailed monitor lizard is on the case in the vast, sandy expanse. With a flick of its super-sniffing tongue, it's gathering clues from the air! Is that the scent of dinner or a fellow lizard nearby? This lizard's tongue is an absolute multitasking marvel, sniffing secrets in the sand!

656. Scuttling along on moonlit nights, dung beetles navigate using the stars above. That's right, the Milky Way guides them, ensuring their precious dung ball is rolled in a straight line, straight away from competitors. Celestial navigators on a moonlit mission!

657. Let's take a stroll through the heart of New York's Central Park. Where the trees echo with the chirps of European starlings. Originally from Europe, these birds are pushing out local birds and causing a scene. A bird with big dreams of taking over in the Big Apple!

658. Time to come out of our shells if we want to meet our next invasive critter. Red-eared slider turtles, native to the southern US, are making surprise appearances in foreign waters, thanks to the pet trade. These unexpected tourists are now hogging the best spots, leaving local turtles in the shade!

659. European beaches are the natural habitat of the green crab. This clever crustacean has made its way into foreign waters by hitching a ride on departing ships. Unfortunately, this crab is causing quite a crabby stir, dining on native shellfish, and stirring the marine pot.

660. Popcorn, corn on the cob, a bit of cornbread... These delicious treats drive Europe to fiercely fight our next menace: the western corn rootworm from Central America. These root-chomping pests are causing a new corn crisis and vastly depleting crops!

661. Fluttering through the dense forests, the male silk moths can catch the faintest whiff of another silk moth. They use this ability to find love, even miles away and then send signals to call them their way. An instinctive way of asking if they'd like to form a future family.

662. Skimming across the rocky shores of New Zealand, we find the mud snail. It might be happy here in New Zealand, but in foreign waters, it's causing chaos, out-eating native species, and disrupting the balance of the ecosystem. A muddy situation, indeed!

663. Swimming back underwater, watch out for a colorful crustacean that packs a punch! The peacock mantis shrimp uses its fast flinging arms to crack open the shells of other crustaceans with a force of approximately 50mph! It's a well-adapted knockout blow every time!

664. Tread carefully, everyone! Hidden in the underbrush, the pit viper waits, its pit organs sensing the warmth of its next meal. Even in the darkest night, the warmth of a mouse or bird shines like a beacon to this cold-blooded predator. Prey doesn't stand a chance against this snake's high-tech radar!

665. Let's trek across the Sahara! The Saharan silver ants shimmer in the sunlight, their silver bodies reflecting the sun's rays. These ants have a built-in sunscreen, allowing them to forage in the scorching heat without getting a sunburn. A unique and mystifying adaptation for such a tiny creature!

666. Grab your shovels and safety glasses, adventurers, and we'll watch how the sand skink burrows! It uses its transparent eyelids to see even while it digs! These built-in goggles let it navigate its sandy realm without a grain of sand touching its eyes. When digging with a sand skink, safety is always first!

667. As we land in the American Southwest, watch your step! Remember our venomous friend, the Gila monster? He's back with another trick up his sleeve! Not only is the Gila monster venomous and adorned with striking patterns, but this multifaceted monster has a battery backup in its tail! Storing fat for times when food is sparse. It's nature's way of preparing for a rainy day!

668. Time for us to meet the spider that knows a thing or two about setting a tricky trap! The Bola spider skulks through the moonlit forests, hunting with a unique tool. Its silk thread is tipped with a sticky blob miming moth pheromones (a chemical scent used by moths to communicate), luring in unsuspecting prey. A showcase of the spider's cunning and precise hunting technique!

669. Farmers markets, beware! US orchards are facing a new threat: the spotted lanternfly from Asia. These sap-sucking pests are feasting on grapes, apples, and hardwood trees, causing ecological and economic concerns. An especially pesky problem for produce lovers!

670. Scuttle along the sandy shores, and you'll spot the fiddler crab, a master of surveillance! With eyes perched on long stalks, these crabs have a nearly 360-degree view, spotting danger from all angles. Even while half-hidden in their burrows, they keep a watchful eye out. It's a crabby lookout, always on high alert!

671. Watch out for the harlequin ladybird, a sneaky invader from eastern Asia! These spotted tricksters are taking over the skies of North America, Europe, and Africa. While they munch on aphids, they're also muscling out the local ladybird populations. It's a real-life drama in the insect world, with these colorful characters playing the lead roles. They might look pretty, but they're causing a stir in the bug community!

672. Let's shrink down to meet the Etruscan shrew, the world's smallest mammal by weight! No bigger than a paperclip and just 1.5 inches long, this tiny dynamo eats twice its body weight in insects daily. With its quick movements, it's a small wonder of nature, showcasing that great things come in tiny packages!

673. Hear that, bird watchers? Asian markets may be alive with the song of the common myna bird. But it's causing quite a ruckus in foreign lands, pushing out local birds and claiming the best spots. A tweeting tyrant, indeed!

674. Grab your bug nets, insect explorers! Next, we will encounter the Emerald ash borer, an Asian glittering beetle. Emerald ash borers are on a destructive spree in North American forests. They're turning lush green canopies into barren landscapes, one tree at a time. That's a giant beetle brunch!

675. Buzzz! Come along, future entomologists. Look in North American backyards, where European paper wasps are flying amok. These stinging invaders are building nests everywhere, causing a painful problem for local wasps. Ouch!

676. Hike with me to see the destruction plaguing the forests in North America. Here, the trees are under siege due to the Asian gypsy moth! Humans are knowingly transferring this fluttering foe. It is now munching away at all the leaves, leaving trees bare and landscapes decimated.

677. Back to North America, we go, where the wood frog has mastered a frosty feat. As winter rolls in, this amphibian becomes a frog-sickle, freezing solid. But don't worry; when spring arrives, it thaws out and leaps back into action. Now, that's what I call extreme hibernation!

678. Ca-cawww! US skies echo the calls of the Eurasian collared dove from Asia and Europe. Due to an unfortunate escape of fewer than 50 birds in captivity in the Bahamas, these winged wanderers are pushing out local species. This has led to a startling shift in the avian balance!

679. All aboard the Curiosity Caboose as we explore an animal with an incredibly cool sense! The mantis shrimp gazes about with eyes that capture a kaleidoscope of colors. With 16 different color channels, they see a world illuminated in ultraviolet and polarized light, making our human vision seem almost monochrome. A rainbow-visioned sea critter!

680. Zap! Our next critter is causing a shockingly significant problem! The southeastern US is crawling with the tawny crazy ants from South America. These rapidly multiplying ants are not only pushing out native ants but also causing significant problems for humans. These pesky problems are even known to infest electronics, causing circuits to short!

681. Woof woof! Our next creature is known as man's best friend for a reason! Bounding through fields and parks, dogs follow a tapestry of scents. Their noses, much more sensitive than ours, tell tales of friends passed by and hidden treats and can even tell the health of those around them. Our playful pooches have a powerful gift!

682. In the heart of the savannah, watch for the caracal, a feline with an extraordinary talent. Known for their distinctive tufted ears, these sleek cats are high-jump experts, leaping up to three meters to catch birds mid-flight. It's a breathtaking display of agility and precision, making the caracal the acrobatic star of the wild. Their leaps aren't just impressive—they're a survival skill turned into an art form!

683. Leap through the leafy canopies of Madagascar with me, where the fossa reigns supreme! This sleek hunter is like a gymnast of the treetops, twisting and turning with cat-like grace, making it among the fastest tree climbers. It's all about the chase, as it zeroes in on speedy lemurs with astonishing agility. A true marvel of adaptation, perfectly poised for the pursuit of its quick-footed quarry!

684. Brace yourselves; this next one's a shocker! In the dense forests of Central Africa, the hairy frog does something straight out of a scary movie. When threatened, it intentionally breaks its own toe bones, pushing them through its skin to form makeshift claws. Talk about a spine-chilling defense!

685. Let's take a look at a spider with an incredibly unique ability! Hiding amongst the leaves, the jumping spider stalks, its eyes capturing the world around it in high definition. With a vision that can detect UV light, they judge distances and pounce with unparalleled accuracy!

686. Timber! Japanese forests are under attack from the variable oakleaf caterpillar, a North American native. These leaf-munching invaders are causing oak trees to shed their leaves, leading to potential tree deaths. Can you imagine something so small causing such considerable destruction?

687. Gear up for a game of hide-and-seek with the ocean's master of disguise, the cuttlefish! Known as the 'chameleon of the sea,' this clever creature's skin is like a magical canvas, shifting colors and patterns in the blink of an eye. It's not just about hiding; this crafty critter uses its skin to express emotions and even send secret signals to other cuttlefish. A fish with a flair for drama and deception!

688. Waders on as we trudge through the swamps of Europe, where the waters are bubbling with activity from the red swamp crayfish! Due to illegal release, this crayfish has spread from the southeastern United States to many areas in Europe. Now, these crustaceans are outcompeting locals for food and habitat. A nasty invader that's reshaping aquatic ecosystems!

689. Now, strap on your climbing gear! We're ascending the misty mountains of the Himalayas. The red panda, with its fiery fur, navigates the treetops among the bamboo thickets. Those sharp claws and a bushy tail for balance make it a nimble acrobat. It's a master of the high ropes, gracefully moving from branch to branch in search of a bamboo feast.

690. Next, let's dive into the waters of Australia! Here, we'll find the platypus, with its duck-bill and webbed feet; it's an expert in detection. It hunts underwater, using its bill to pick up the electrical signals of its prey. It's like a built-in food detector!

691. Get your hedge trimmers ready! Let's venture into a southern garden, where Kudzu, the vine from East Asia, was planted with pride. But this ambitious climber dreamed of being the best, overshadowing and overtaking everything in its path. A plant with a plan to rise to the top!

692. Watch out, adventurers, we are about to meet a lizard with a sneaky skill! Found in the deserts of North America, the horned lizard hides a disgusting ability fit for a horror movie! When cornered, it can squirt blood from its eyes, giving predators a taste they won't soon forget. It's the ultimate "back off" signal!

693. Forage the dense underbrush of New Zealand with the kiwi! No, not the fruit, the bird! Kiwis use their nostrils to probe the ground. With nostrils situated at the tip of their beaks, they can easily sniff out worms and insects. A bird with a beak that can make a buffet!

694. Time to set sail and brave the waves to meet the quagga mussel. This invasive invertebrate hails from Eastern Europe but has made its way to North American waters by stowing away in cargo ships' ballasts, hulls, motors, and pipes. These filter feeders are reshaping aquatic ecosystems and causing problems for local industries. A traveling tyrant, indeed!

WACKY WORDS & SCIENTIFIC SURPRISES

695. Step back in time, young explorers! We are about to enter the bustling labs of the 1920s with Ivan Pavlov! He demonstrated how dogs could learn that the sound of a bell meant food was coming. This is known now as "classical conditioning." It's a groundbreaking exploration of learning and behavior!

696. Teleporting: science fiction or future reality? Quantum teleportation involves the instantaneous transfer of information at a quantum level. This fascinating field of study could revolutionize how we understand and transmit data.

697. Let's flap our wings back to the 1950s with B.F. Skinner! He had a quirky idea: teaching pigeons to play ping pong! He used treats and tricks to guide their behavior, a method called operant conditioning. It's like training pets with snacks and praise. A fun flap through the world of behavioral science!

698. Imagine scaling walls effortlessly! Scientists, inspired by the wall-climbing prowess of geckos, are developing adhesives that replicate their ability. This innovation will soon enable us to ascend vertical surfaces as effortlessly.

699. Echo-Echo! Did you hear that?-Did you hear that? We are hearing an echo, explorers! Echoes are your voice going on an adventurous journey. When you shout, your voice travels until it hits a wall or a mountain and then races back to your ears. It's like your voice is playing a game of tag with itself!

700. Think you could outrun a car? Humans can't match super speeds, but Usain Bolt, the fastest man, achieved a speed of 27.8 mph. This extraordinary display of human velocity shows us our limits and capabilities.

701. Be awestruck by 'ineffable,' the immense beauty that leaves you lost for words. It's like standing on top of a mountain, gazing at a view so magnificent that all you can do is gasp in wonder. 'Ineffable' is the feeling when something is so extraordinary that words just can't do it justice!

702. Click! Our eyes are like super-powered cameras. They capture light, turn it into electrical signals, and send it to our brains, creating the images we see. The human body's portal straight to our brain!

703. Navigate the neuro-wonders with Roger Sperry in the 1960s! He embarked on a cerebral safari, discovering how our brain's hemispheres have unique talents. The left side excels in logic and language, while the right is a master of creativity and intuition. It's a mind-bending journey through the fascinating landscapes of our brains!

704. Embark on an atomic adventure, particle pioneers! In the early 1900s, Ernest Rutherford made a tiny but huge discovery: the atomic nucleus, where protons and neutrons live. Think of an atom as a miniature solar system, with a nucleus at the center like the sun! It's a journey to the very heart of matter itself!

705. Let's answer the age-old question: Why is the sky blue? It's all thanks to tiny air molecules playing with the sun's light. They scatter the blue part of sunlight all around the sky, painting it in that lovely hue. So next time you look up, remember it's a giant, natural canvas!

706. Play with 'tmesis,' the linguistic jigsaw where words are split and reassembled. It's a fun twist of language, like cutting up sentences and piecing them back in surprising new ways, a creative tango of words!

707. Unravel the enigma of 'cryptomnesia,' the mind's own game of hide-and-seek with memories. It's like rediscovering an old idea as if it's brand new, a trick where your brain plays the magician, pulling forgotten thoughts out of its hat!

708. Did you know chefs are an exceptional kind of scientist? Indeed, cooking is like conducting a delicious science experiment! Heat changes the food, transforming its flavor, texture, and appearance. It's a magical process that turns simple ingredients into mouth-watering dishes!

709. Gear up, disease detectives! We're heading to the 1840s with John Snow. He unraveled a health mystery in London, linking a cholera outbreak to a single contaminated water source. His work laid the foundation for the modern study of disease, changing how we tackle public health challenges. A real life-saving expedition!

710. What if you could shrink down to a tiny size? Nanotechnology lets us manipulate materials on an incredibly small scale – as minuscule as one billionth of a meter. This groundbreaking science opens doors to myriad innovations, from medicine to electronics.

711. Grab your tennis balls and meet me at the courts! Ready, set, throw! When you bounce a ball, it's like watching a dance of energy. The ball squishes and springs back, changing its power from one form to another. It's a lively display of physics in action, right in your hands!

712. Discover the charm of 'lagniappe,' the wonderful surprise of getting a bit more than you bargained for! It's like unwrapping a gift and finding an extra treat hidden inside or getting an unexpected bonus just because. These little extras bring joy to your day, making ordinary moments a bit more special!

713. Meet 'Agelast,' the enigma who travels life's path without the music of laughter. It's a solemn journey, a reminder that joy wears many faces and not all are marked by smiles, a reflection of the vast tapestry of human feelings.

714. Have you ever wondered why your shadow follows you around? Shadows are made when something blocks light, casting a dark shape. The size and shape of the shadow depend on the light and the object, as well as the distance of the object from the light. Thanks to a trick of the light, your shadow will always follow you!

715. Wish you could change color to match your mood? Chameleons do just that! Their ability to change skin color for communication and camouflage is one of nature's most fascinating adaptations, a real-life superpower in the animal kingdom.

716. Step into the animal kingdom with Konrad Lorenz, our guide to the 20th century! He uncovered the secret of imprinting, where baby animals think the first moving thing they see is their parent. Imagine ducklings following a bouncing ball as if it's their mom! It's a fascinating waddle through the wonders of animal behavior!

717. How cool would it be to see through walls? X-ray machines use electromagnetic waves to peer inside objects, offering us a glimpse into a world hidden from the naked eye, much like the fantastical power of X-ray vision.

718. Get ready to feel 'aquiver,' the shivery thrill of waiting for something unique to happen! It's like the flutter of butterfly wings in your stomach just before something exciting, like the countdown to your birthday party. It's all about that tingly, jittery joy of looking forward to something fantastic!

719. Magnet power at your fingertips! Electromagnets, capable of lifting heavy objects and integral to MRI machines, showcase the immense power of magnetism. They represent a real-world application of what seems like a magnetic superpower.

720. Listen closely as we explore the experience of sound! Sound is made and transported through vibrations that send waves through the air. Our ears catch these waves and turn them into sounds we can hear. Sound is the sense that we can sometimes feel and hear!

721. Ponder 'velleity,' the softest echo of a wish that barely stirs the air. It's like a feather-light dream that flutters into your mind, only to vanish before it turns into a natural desire, a wisp of a thought that's here and then gone.

722. How many times have you opened a bottle of glue and used it without ever questioning how it works? Glue uses the power of adhesion to stick things together! Its molecules grab onto the surface and stick to themselves, creating a strong bond. It's like having a superpower that makes things stick with just a touch!

723. Laser vision – wouldn't that be a sight? Lasers in the real world, capable of cutting through metal, play crucial roles in surgeries and manufacturing. They represent our closest equivalent to the focused intensity of a superhero's gaze.

724. Step into the world of light and reflections with mirrors! Mirrors are like magical portals that capture and throw light back at us, creating perfect copies of whatever stands before them. It's as if they're saying, "Here's your twin from the land of reflection!"

725. Walk with 'somnambulist,' the silent voyager of the night. In the realm of sleepwalking, the body embarks on its own nocturnal adventures while the mind drifts in the land of dreams, a mysterious ballet of sleep and motion.

726. Next, we're taking a deep breath in the 18th century with Joseph Priestley! He unveiled the secret of the air we breathe – oxygen! This discovery showed how this vital gas fuels life. It's like finding an invisible key to unlock one of the secrets of life. A scientific breath of fresh air!

727. Get out your bubble wands and learn about the magic of bubbles! When water and soap come together, they create a thin skin that traps air, forming bubbles. These shimmering spheres float and dance in the air like tiny, glistening balloons. A sensation with a scientific twist!

728. Leap into 'alacrity,' the bright spark of being ready at a moment's notice. It's the rush of excitement when jumping into action, a burst of energy fueled by the joy of helping, a sprint of enthusiasm to make a difference!

729. Imagine having bat-like super hearing! Bats navigate the night using echolocation, a remarkable natural ability that allows them to 'see' their surroundings through sound, an extraordinary demonstration of nature's ingenuity.

730. Grab your popcorn! In the 1940s and 1950s, Barbara McClintock made a groundbreaking discovery in cornfields. She found 'jumping genes' – bits of DNA that can move around and switch up an organism's traits. Imagine genes playing a game of musical chairs inside corn! It's a kernel-popping adventure in the world of genetic innovation!

731. Next, we're returning to the 19th century to meet the brilliant Michael Faraday! He shared with the world his groundbreaking work in electromagnetic induction. He discovered that a moving magnet could create an electric current, magically turning magnetism into electricity. It's a thrilling adventure through the electrifying and magnetic mysteries of science!

732. We all know the sun is the star of nature's show, but why? Not only is it giving us light and warmth, but it also powers life on earth and influences our weather. It's like the sun is the conductor of a giant orchestra, directing everything on our planet!

733. Dive into the science of staying cool! When we sweat, our bodies are unleashing their own natural air conditioning. As the sweat evaporates, it whisks away heat like tiny droplets carrying away warmth on their invisible wings.

734. Discover 'zarf', the unsung hero of your hot cocoa adventures. The trusty sleeve lets you hold a steaming cup without a wince, a guardian against the heat, turning a scalding moment into a warm, comfortable sip!

735. Ever seen a human pretzel? Contortionists' incredible flexibility demonstrates the astonishing limits of the human body. Through a combination of genetics and rigorous training, they achieve feats that seem to defy physical boundaries.

736. Huuummm! Sorry explorers, I seem a little tired and can't stop yawning! Here's a fun fact: yawning might help cool our brains or provide them with extra oxygen when tired or bored. However, the big mystery scientists are still sleeping on is why a yawn is contagious! Yawning is like having a sleepy signal that spreads from person to person.

737. Airplanes, those giant metal birds in the sky, stay up thanks to the clever shape of their wings. The wings are designed to push air down and create lift, letting the plane rise. It's like a magic trick, but with physics!

738. Look up to the night sky for a chemistry spectacular! Fireworks are like artists painting the sky with light. Each color bursts forth from different chemicals burning at scorching temperatures. It's a dazzling display of science lighting up the heavens!

739. Have you ever played with magnets and wondered why they stick together or push apart? It's because of invisible magnetic fields created by the movement of electric charges. These fields are like secret forces, making magnets attract or repel each other. Holding a set of magnets feels like having invisible powers in your hands!

740. Fine-tune your ears to the gentle whispers of 'susurrus,' the soothing sounds that nature murmurs. It's like the hush-hush of leaves dancing in the wind or the soft babble of a brook, all speaking in nature's calm and peaceful language. These sounds wrap you in a blanket of serenity, inviting you to listen to the quiet symphony of the great outdoors.

741. Look to the sky, future astronomers! Do you see that twinkling? It's the stars! Stars twinkle because their light bends as it passes through earth's atmosphere. It's like the stars are winking at us from afar, each twinkling a secret message from the depths of space!

742. Leap into the lucky land of 'serendipity,' where surprises await you! It's like going on a treasure hunt and finding a hidden gem by accident. Imagine finding a cool rock or a shiny coin when you're not even looking – that's 'serendipity' for you!

743. Step into the cheesy paradise of 'turophile,' where every slice and wedge is a delight. It's a journey through the land of creamy, tangy, and sharp delights, a celebration of all things cheese, from the softest brie to the boldest blue!

744. Enter the buzzing world of microwaves, where cooking is a high-speed dance! Inside the microwave, tiny water molecules in your food vibrate super fast, creating heat. It's like each molecule is doing a fiery tango, heating up your meal from the inside out!

745. Zap! Are you ready for a shocking fact? Static electricity is like a sneaky spark waiting to jump. When different materials rub together, they swap electrons, building up an electric charge. Then, zap! A mini lightning bolt leaps out, giving you a surprising little jolt!

746. If you had a jetpack, where would you fly? Jetpacks let us zoom through the air at exhilarating speeds of over 30 mph and reach awe-inspiring heights of up to 3,000 feet. It's our closest real-life approach to soaring like the birds!

747. Look up at the moon, shining down on us at night. But did you know the moon doesn't shine its own light? In fact, it reflects the sun's light like a giant cosmic mirror in the night sky. So, when you see the moon glowing, it's the sun's light dressed in moonlight, playing a game of cosmic catch.

748. Get ready to light up your minds as we're charging into the 20th century with the brilliant Nikola Tesla. He was a master of electricity, inventing the alternating current that powers our homes today. Tesla even dreamed of sending messages through the airway before Wi-Fi! It's a high-voltage voyage through the bright sparks of innovation!

749. Ever wonder why ice floats in your glass of water rather than sinking to the bottom? Well, that's because the ice in your drink is lighter than water. When water turns into ice, it expands and becomes less dense, allowing it to bob on the surface. It's like a magic trick right in your cup!

750. Inhale the fresh scent of 'petrichor,' nature's fragrance that comes alive after the rain. The earth is taking a deep, refreshing breath, filling the air with a clean, green smell that makes everything feel new again. Imagine the aroma of wet soil and rain-washed leaves – that's 'petrichor' for you, a breath of fresh air!

751. Imagine the sky turning into a giant, colorful arc after a storm. That's the magic of rainbows! When sunlight meets raindrops, it bends and splits into a spectrum of colors. Each
color takes a different path, creating that beautiful, colorful bow. It's like nature's own painting in the sky!

752. Hold on tight for a gravity-defying journey! Roller coasters are like dragons of steel and speed, using the laws of physics to take us on a wild ride. They zoom and loop, powered by gravity and kinetic energy, turning the world into a blur of excitement!

753. Marvel at 'clinquant,' the shimmering spectacle of all that glitters and gleams. It's the world dressed in its finest sparkles, where the ordinary becomes extraordinary under a shower of radiant light.

754. Immerse yourself in the sparkling world of 'mirth,' a place where laughter shines bright and happiness is contagious. It's like a burst of sunshine in the form of giggles and grins, spreading cheer and lifting everyone's spirits. 'Mirth' is the magical laughter that can turn any space into a room full of joy and light!

755. Soap cleans by containing one set of molecules that love water and another that love dirt! Mix them together, and you get sudsy sanitation! This combo also lets soap grab grease and wash it away. It's like having a tiny superhero that fights dirt and grime!

756. Explore 'apraxia,' the puzzling gap where thoughts and actions don't quite connect. It's like having the map but finding the roads untraveled, a challenging dance where the mind leads but the body hesitates.

757. An invisibility cloak – now that would be a game-changer! Research into light-bending materials might one day enable objects to become unseen, a step closer to the mystical world of invisibility.

758. Soil, water, and sunshine! These ingredients are needed to grow a healthy plant, but how does the plant use sunlight? Plants are like nature's solar panels. They use sunlight to make their food through a process called photosynthesis, turning light into energy. It's like cooking but with sunlight as the main ingredient!

759. Ever seen leaves spiraling in the wind? This dance is caused by vortices, swirling air patterns formed by the wind's playful push and pull. It's like nature's merry-go-round, twirling leaves in a whimsical waltz!

760. Brrrr, is it a bit cold in here? When we shiver, our bodies are trying to warm up. Our muscles rapidly shake, creating heat to keep us cozy. It's like having a built-in heater that turns on automatically when cold!

761. Sign 'hello' to Koko the gorilla, our remarkable friend from the 1980s! Koko learned American Sign Language, using her hands to communicate just like humans. She showed the world how gorillas can express their thoughts and feelings, opening our eyes to the amazing world of non-verbal communication. A sign that even without words, we can share our world and our hearts.

762. Time to don your lab coats; we're mixing it up in the 1700s with Antoine Lavoisier! He's the brain behind modern chemistry, sorting out chemicals and uncovering their secrets like that water is H_2O – two hydrogen atoms bonded with one oxygen atom! A bubbling adventure through the building blocks of everything!

763. Ever wonder why the ocean is so salty that we can't even drink it? It's because of minerals washed down from rocks on land. It's like the sea is a giant soup, seasoned over millions of years by the earth's ingredients!

764. Why do volcanoes erupt with such power? The intense heat causes so much pressure to build up deep within the earth that it is eventually forced to go up and out! It's like the planet exploding with a destructive molten display!

765. Time to be amazed by the magnificent sight of the Northern and Southern Lights (or auroras)! These auroras are caused by solar particles colliding with the earth's atmosphere. It's like the sky is a giant canvas, with the sun painting it with light brushes!

766. Who hasn't dreamed of turning invisible? Scientists are exploring materials that bend light, inching closer to making objects vanish from sight. This fascinating field of research could one day bring the fantasy of invisibility to life!

767. How fast can you run? The world's fastest sprinters, like Usain Bolt, push the limits of human speed, showcasing our incredible potential for speed and agility in a display of awe-inspiring athleticism.

768. Click, say cheese, and freeze! Cameras are like time-freezing wizards. They capture the light like our eyes and hold onto it, creating a picture. It's like having the power to stop time and keep a piece of it with you forever!

769. Dive into the delightful world of 'mellifluous,' where every sound is as sweet as honey! It's like listening to a gentle stream of music that tickles your ears and makes your heart smile. Imagine the soft strumming of a guitar or the peaceful chirping of birds at dawn – that's the beauty of 'mellifluous'!

770. Untangle the wordy knot of 'gobbledygook,' a jumble of words that seems like a riddle. It's like trying to solve a puzzle of sentences, where each piece is a word that needs to find its place. Deciphering 'gobbledygook' is like being a language detective, cracking the code of confusion!

771. Yellow, orange, purple, blue! Butterflies can be found in almost every color! Most might expect that their vibrant colors come from only their pigments, but their color can also be determined by the structure of their wings. Each wing is a microscopic kaleidoscope, reflecting light in dazzling patterns!

772. Imagine suiting up in an exoskeleton! These advanced suits, designed to augment human strength, are paving the way for us to lift heavy loads easily and assist in rehabilitation, much like wearing a suit of superhuman strength.

773. Buzz into the world of heredity with Thomas Hunt Morgan! In the early 20th century, he turned tiny fruit flies into the real superstars of science. By studying these buzzing creatures, he was able to unlock the secrets of genetics and inheritance. One tiny (but significant) wing flap for mankind!

774. Ever seen rainbows in oil puddles? The thin film of the oil causes light to pass through and bounce back differently off the water underneath! This is just light showing off its colorful side, like a mini light show on the ground!

775. Venture into the odd world of 'schadenfreude,' where seeing someone else's goof-ups is surprisingly fun. It's a weird, cheeky feeling, like trying not to giggle when someone trips over their feet – as long as they're okay! It's a funny and human emotion, finding humor in life's clumsy moments.

776. How about your own energy shield? Research in plasma-based shields aims to protect against space radiation, a step closer to creating personal force fields that could safeguard astronauts on their cosmic journeys.

777. Embark on an exhilarating escapade with 'wanderlust,' the irresistible urge to roam and discover! It's like being a treasure hunter of experiences, craving adventures in lands far and wide and soaking up the wonders of diverse cultures!

778.
Encounter 'snollygoster,' the sly fox of the political jungle. It's all about being cunning and clever, sometimes bending the rules to win the game. Imagine a chess player who's always two steps ahead; that's a 'snollygoster' for you

779. – smart, but maybe a little too sneaky!

Fancy being a detective with high-tech tools? Forensic science, employing techniques like DNA analysis, is the real-world counterpart to the skills of the greatest fictional detectives, unraveling mysteries one clue at a time.

780. Strap in, space explorers! We're rocketing to the stars with Sally Ride in 1983! She made history as the first American woman to venture into space, shattering the glass ceiling in science and space exploration. Blazing a trail for future generations in the endless expanse of the universe!

781. Healing at super speed is a handy ability! While instant healing remains in comic books, research into the human liver's regenerative capacity and animals like salamanders offer insights into potential regenerative abilities in humans.

782. Freezing things in an instant – cool, right? Liquid nitrogen enables scientists to flash-freeze objects at a bone-chilling -320°F. This technology, straight out of a sci-fi novel, is a crucial tool in fields like cryogenics and food preservation.

783. Jump through the leaves in autumn! This time of year, trees put on a spectacular color show. They stop making the green chlorophyll, letting hidden colors in the leaves shine through. The trees are throwing their own fall fashion show, with leaves dressed in vibrant reds, oranges, and yellows.

784. 3D printers – the next best thing to materializing objects from air! This technology enables the creation of a wide range of items, from playful toys to life-saving prosthetics, layer by layer. It's a modern form of alchemy, transforming digital designs into tangible realities.

785. Grab those microscopes; we're spiraling through the 1950s with James Watson and Francis Crick! With help from data shared by Rosalind Franklin, they unveiled the structure of DNA as being like a twisted ladder known as a double helix. This twist holds the secret code of life; from your hair color to your height, it's the blueprint of you!

786. Electricity is like a super-fast race of tiny particles called electrons. When you flip a switch, you're letting these tiny racers flow through wires, bringing light and power to everything around you. It's like unleashing a tiny lightning bolt at your fingertips!

787. Sail into the swirling seas of 'bumfuzzle,' where everything seems topsy-turvy and confusing. It's like finding yourself in a maze of questions, scratching your head, and wondering which way to turn. Imagine being baffled by a magician's trick – that's the feeling of being 'bumfuzzled,' completely mystified by life's little puzzles!

788. Listen for the magical melody of 'tintinnabulation,' the enchanting jingle of bells ringing through the air! It's like being surrounded by a choir of tiny bells, each one chiming in to create a joyful harmony that dances around you. Imagine the twinkling sound of wind chimes on a breezy day – that's the charm of 'tintinnabulation'!

789. Ever wondered about superhuman strength? The world record for weightlifting is a jaw-dropping 1,100 pounds. This feat of strength, achieved through intense training, is the pinnacle of human physical prowess, a testament to what dedication and grit can accomplish.

790. Breathing underwater like a fish – fancy a swim? Scuba diving technology allows us to explore the ocean's depths, with the record for the deepest scuba dive reaching over 1,000 feet. It's our version of an aquatic adventure into the unknown.

791. Reading minds – now that would be a trick! Developing brain-computer interfaces might one day allow us to communicate through our thoughts alone. This cutting-edge technology is a step towards what was once considered the realm of telepathy.

792. And now for a moldy mystery! In 1928, Alexander Fleming made a life-saving discovery by accident. He found that a mold called penicillin could defeat dangerous bacteria. Penicillin is still used around the world today! It was like finding a superhero in a petri dish! An amazing antibiotic adventure!

793. Get ready for a magnetic adventure! Compasses are like secret agents of the earth, always pointing north. They align with earth's magnetic field, a hidden force that wraps around our planet. It's like having an invisible guide whispering, "This way to the North Pole!"

794. Taming lightning – a shocking idea! By safely grounding this natural electric force, lightning rods protect buildings and lives, demonstrating a clever use of one of nature's most formidable powers.

795. Trek through the harsh desert, but remember your water bottle! Unlike the cacti, we need to stay constantly hydrated! Cacti survive in harsh deserts by storing water in their thick stems. It's like they're nature's own water bottles, cleverly designed to thrive in the driest places!

796. Behold the fleeting world of 'ephemeral,' where beauty lasts only for a moment, like a flash of fireworks in the night sky. It's about those precious, short-lived moments that take your breath away – like the last glow of a sunset or the swift streak of a shooting star. These are the 'ephemeral' wonders, here for an instant, but leaving a lasting memory in your heart!

797. Harnessing the power of stars – a stellar concept! Nuclear fusion research is delving into replicating the sun's energy process, potentially unlocking a future of clean, limitless power, a venture as ambitious as reaching for the stars.

INNOVATIVE BREAKTHROUGHS & ACCIDENTAL DISCOVERIES

798. Strap on your flight goggles! We're about to join the animal air pioneers of 1783 in their historic balloon journey! On September 19, 1783, the skies witnessed a peculiar sight – a sheep, a duck, and a rooster soaring through the air in a hot air balloon! This whimsical trio wasn't just enjoying the view; they were the first brave souls (or feathers and wool) to test the effects of flight on living beings. A baa-ck-quacking adventure indeed!

799. Do you smell something sweet, future scientists? Chemist Constantin Fahlberg sure did; after a day in the lab, he tasted something unexpectedly sweet on his fingers. He hadn't washed his hands! This accidental encounter led to the discovery of saccharin, the zero-calorie sweetener. Sweet serendipity, indeed!

800. Zap! Here's a striking fact: New York's Empire State Building is a magnet for lightning! This beacon of the Manhattan skyline is struck by lightning about 23 times yearly. Each strike is a shocking and dramatic display of nature's power that electrifies the city's heartbeat.

801. Stick around and hear about Roy Plunkett. Plunkett was aiming for a new refrigerant, but instead, he slipped and slid into the discovery of Teflon, the non-stick marvel. It's fascinating how some discoveries just, well, stick!

802. Look at those sails, explorers! No, that's no boat; it's a building with sails! The Sydney Opera House, with its iconic sails, isn't just an architectural marvel; it's a self-cleaning wonder. Over 1 million glossy tiles cover its roofs, repelling dirt and grime, proving that beauty can sometimes be low maintenance.

803. Learn about life-saving mistakes with Wilson Greatbatch. The tiny error of inserting the wrong resistor transformed a heart-rhythm recording device into a life-saving pacemaker! It's heartwarming how some errors can set the right rhythm for innovations.

804. Grab your tickets and find a seat on the London Eye, a giant ferris wheel of wonder! This 443-foot attraction offers breathtaking views! Anchored in the River Thames, its foundations lie underwater, a hidden strength beneath the flowing currents. A perfect blend of aquatic engineering and sky-high thrills!

805. Here we go! Step onto the conveyor belt for humans and meet the first moving sidewalk! An early version of the airport transportation system we use today was introduced in 1893 at the Chicago World's Fair. A stroll through history, this invention was an exciting step towards the future of pedestrian mobility!

806. Let's look up high in the sky, future architects! The Bahrain World Trade Center isn't just reaching for the skies; it's harnessing the wind. With integrated wind turbines, this skyscraper is a swirling dance of renewable energy, a pioneering giant in eco-friendly architecture. An innovative skyscraper that is setting the bar high for sustainable skyscrapers!

807. Grab your tie-dye shirts in honor of William Perkin, who, at just 18, was trying to synthesize quinine. Instead, he ended up with a vibrant dye, giving the world its first taste of synthetic color: mauve. Sometimes, the best results are different from what you're aiming for!

808. Hop aboard our imaginary plane to Paris! We're off to witness the Eiffel Tower's astounding summer growth spurt! This architectural feat isn't just a feast for the eyes; it's a marvel of thermal expansion! This iron giant can stretch up to 6 inches taller in the summer heat. A monument that grows up, even if just for a season!

809. Take a snapshot of your skeleton with Wilhelm Conrad Roentgen! Who stumbled upon the mysterious X-ray when he spotted a fluorescent glow near a cathode-ray tube (a vital part used in old TV manufacturing). This accidental glow illuminated medical science, changing diagnostics forever!

810. Every time you grab a frozen treat on a hot summer day, you have Young Frank Epperson to thank. Epperson left a liquid mixture outside overnight in 1905. The chilly morning gifted him—and the world—the popsicle. A frosty accident that melted hearts!

811. Grab your walking shoes and join me on a sightseeing tour of the Akashi Kaikyo Bridge! Located in Japan, it isn't just a bridge; it's a record-breaking stretch of ingenuity. With the longest central span of any suspension bridge, it's a testament to human ambition, spanning not just water but the realms of possibility. These architects are truly "truss-ing" their innovative designs.

812. Hope you aren't afraid of heights, adventurers! We're about to travel along France's Millau Viaduct, a bridge higher than the Eiffel Tower. At over 1,125 feet, it is the tallest of its kind and a testament to the heights of human aspiration. It's genuinely like a ribbon running through the clouds.

813. Opening the refrigerator to grab an icy drink or an appetizing snack seems like such an easy task, doesn't it? However, keeping food and drink cool was once a huge hassle! Thanks to Thomas Midgley Jr., who was trying to create a new cooling agent, we now have one of life's most valuable tools...Freon! Freon has changed the world, becoming the world's first widely used refrigerant.

814. Can you dance through an earthquake? Ancient Japanese pagodas sure can! Uniquely designed with central swaying pillars, they are marvels of seismic engineering. This fantastic design has lasted the test of time, helping keep the building and people inside safe. Brainy builders of the past certainly knew their stuff!

815. Dive into a hidden underwater world! Beneath the waves, we'll uncover the secret superhighway of submarine communications cables. The submarine information superhighway carries over 99% of international data. These underwater highways are the unsung heroes of our global internet, silently streaming cat videos and emails across the deep blue.

816. Stand back! Henri Becquerel's work was dangerous but incredibly illuminating! His work on phosphorescent materials radiated into the discovery of radioactivity. It's electrifying how some discoveries can glow with potential!

817. Grab a glass of milk, and bake with Ruth Wakefield. Wakefield's cookie experiment took a chocolaty turn when she added chocolate chunks, thinking they'd completely melt. The result? The world's first chocolate chip cookie. A delicious twist of fate!

818. Let's find out what's cooking with engineer Percy Spencer! While working on radar equipment, Spencer felt a peculiar warmth. A candy bar in his pocket had melted, leading to the birth of the microwave oven. Sometimes, life's little accidents can heat things up in unexpected ways!

819. From applicable invention to silly sensation, the world welcomed Silly Putty! During World War II, engineers aimed to create synthetic rubber but ended up with Silly Putty. It's a stretchy reminder that sometimes, you bounce in unexpected directions.

820. Do you feel that, adventurers? The Golden Gate Bridge is swaying beneath our feet! San Francisco's Golden Gate Bridge isn't just a pretty landmark; it's a master of flexibility. Propelled by strong winds, this bridge can sway up to 27 feet from side to side; That's like the length of two school buses lined up front to back! It's a testament to engineering that moves with nature, quite literally!

821. Who knew something designed to clean would end up being one of the world's most loved toys! During a failed attempt to create a new wallpaper-cleaning agent, Noah McVicker and Joseph McVicker invented Play-Doh. A reminder to always keep using your imagination to create new things!

822. Say cheese! Thanks to Joseph Nicéphore Niépce, we gained the gift of capturing those smiles. Niépce was on a quest to make an efficient lithography (or printing machine) and instead managed to capture the world's first photograph. A picture-perfect accident that framed history!

823. Walk with George de Mestral, where, on a hike, he observed burrs clinging to his dog's fur. This sticky situation inspired the creation of Velcro, proving that nature often has the best hooks for innovation!

824. Shhh! Let's listen to the secrets of the ancient Romans. They weren't just building an empire; they were mastering the art of concrete. Their secret? Possibly volcanic ash, making their structures strong and enduring through millennia. A mystery that still has scientists scratching their heads in awe.

825. Pack your bags for a culinary adventure! We're trekking along the Great Wall of China to discover a sticky secret that's held it together for centuries! Parts of this ancient fortress were held together by a sticky rice mortar. Yes, you heard it right – sticky rice! This secret ingredient has been the wall's steadfast ally for centuries, proving that sometimes, the kitchen holds the key to architectural wonders. A sticky solution that saved the day!

826. Grab those telescopes, explorers, and discover the solar system with William Herschel. While mapping stars, he landed on something unexpected: the planet Uranus! It's a cosmic reminder that sometimes, the universe has its own plans!

827. Let's soak up some sun with France's sunlit superhighway! This particular road is more than just a path; it is a beacon of renewable energy. This highway allows France to lead the way in providing solar power to light local streetlamps! Illuminating the way forward, it's a journey towards a brighter, more sustainable future.

828. Grab your bikes, and let's pedal along the SolaRoad In the Netherlands, a bike path that isn't just a path; it's a power station! Embedded with solar panels, this innovative trail harnesses the sun's energy, lighting the way for a greener, cleaner future. Pedal power meets solar power!

829. Let's prepare to see a bridge that seemingly never ends! The Danyang-Kunshan Grand Bridge in China isn't just a bridge; it's an engineering marvel stretching over 102 miles. This colossal structure is a testament to human ingenuity, proving that no distance is too far when connecting people!

830. The Hoover Dam certainly is an incredible sight, but did you know that engineers didn't find it so cool? This fantastic feat of concrete and ambition faced a unique challenge – its own heat! It would have taken 125 years to cool if poured in one go. Instead, engineers poured it in blocks, a jigsaw puzzle of epic proportions, ensuring this monumental dam didn't turn into a monumental oven!

831. Grab your ice skates and glide over to Sweden's Ice Palaces! Here, seasonal hotels are not just built but sculpted from ice and snow! Nearly everything in these mesmerizing wonders is carved from ice, even the beds! Then, each spring, these chiseled castles melt back into the river. These icy abodes are a fleeting dance of frost and art, here today and gone with the thaw.

832. Imagine Édouard Bénédictus's surprise when he dropped a bottle, which didn't shatter. This bottle just so happened to be coated with plastic cellulose nitrate. This mixture not only kept his floors clear of shattered glass, but it paved the way for the invention of safety glass! This accident proved that there's no use crying over a dropped bottle!

833. Leave a note with Spencer Silver. Silver once aimed for a super-strong adhesive at 3M but landed on the opposite end: a weak one. But this "mistake" stuck around, giving us the indispensable Post-it Notes. Sometimes, not sticking to the plan works out!

834. Grab a snack with our next incidental inventor, Chef George Crum! His sarcastic response to a customer's complaint about thick fries crisped into the world's first potato chips. A crunchy comeback that became a snack sensation!

835. Come along, zig-zag with me through Lombard Street in San Francisco! With its eight hairpin turns, it is more than just a road; it's a serpentine spectacle. Designed to tame a steep slope, it's a zig-zagging journey through one of the city's most picturesque neighborhoods. A harrowing hairpin home on the hills!

836. Do you smell that, explorers? After spending a lot of time and money to find a more stable rubber, something is burning in Charles Goodyear's kitchen. Goodyear accidentally dropped a mixture of rubber and sulfur on a hot stove. The result was vulcanized rubber (a more durable and elastic material), and a dream was finally realized!

837. Fly high with the Wright Brothers! Orville and Wilbur Wright were actually bicycle manufacturers before they soared into history. Their curiosity and mechanical skills, honed from bicycles, propelled them to build and fly the world's first successful motor-operated airplane. A leap from pedals to propellers that changed travel forever!

838. Let's step onto the suspension bridges of the Inca Empire. These engineering marvels were woven from grass. Incredibly, some are still in use today, making them a testament to sustainable construction and the enduring ingenuity of the Inca civilization.

839. Have you ever played with a slinky and wondered how it was created? Wonder no more! When naval engineer Richard James knocked a spring off a shelf, he didn't just see it fall—he watched it "walk." That little tumble gave the world the playful Slinky toy, a childhood favorite that dances down the stairs.

840. Grab your oars, and let's board our canoes. Because it's time to float through Bangladesh to see an inspirational innovation in gardening! Brilliant farmers turn adversity into innovation with floating gardens. Made of water hyacinth and bamboo, these buoyant beds of greenery are a testament to human resilience and ingenuity, thriving in the flood seasons.

841. Are you ready to climb 2,909 stairs? Or perhaps we'll take the elevator to see the top of Dubai's towering Burj Khalifa. After climbing a few ladders, you'll find the roof especially sunny! This enormous building isn't just scraping the sky; it's stealing extra sunlight! Standing over 2,700 feet tall, this architectural giant enjoys up to 15 extra minutes of sunshine at its top compared to its base. A literal 'sunny side up' for the highest floors!

842. Did you know, world explorers, that the Leaning Tower of Pisa was never meant to lean? It was a major architectural oopsie! The lean of this 8-story building began when it was accidentally built on soft ground, which caused it to gradually start leaning. A reminder that sometimes, our mistakes can become our most significant works of art!

843. Sometimes, a messy accident is actually a discovery in disguise! One day, a hot soldering iron met an ink pen in the hands of a Canon engineer. The result? Ink ejected! From this, the inkjet printer concept was born! It's incredible how a little spill can lead to a splash of innovation.

844. Skip a rock across the water as we journey back to 1947. Where a Bedouin shepherd's stone toss echoed with the sound of breaking pottery. This chance throw unveiled the Dead Sea Scrolls, unrolling pages of ancient history.

845. Yum! Grab a taste of America's favorite treat: ice cream! At the 1904 World's Fair, an ice cream vendor ran out of dishes. To solve this problem, he teamed up with a waffle vendor, and the delightful ice cream cone was born. A sweet solution to a chilly problem!

846. Stick around and learn about how a sticky project went astray! During a failed experiment to create a new adhesive, Harry Coover discovered the super-strong properties of cyanoacrylate. This happy accident led to the invention of Super Glue!

847. Remember that time you were running a fever? Feeling a bit chilly? Thanks to Daniel Fahrenheit's accidental invention, we can undoubtedly check how our body resounds when we feel under the weather! Although thermometers have evolved for safety reasons, Fahrenheit made a groundbreaking discovery when trying to develop a new type of thermometer. The result was the creation of the first mercury-in-glass thermometer!

THE SMELLY, STRANGE & THE SENSATIONAL

848. Hold onto your noses! The durian fruit from Southeast Asia certainly is a doozy. Known as the "King of Fruits," its aroma is so potent it's banned in some places! But for every nose that wrinkles, a taste bud dances. A fragrant mystery wrapped in spiky armor!

849. High among the treetops of Central and South America, the three-toed sloth wears its musk like a cloak of invisibility. This slow-moving creature releases its musk to ward off predators and blend seamlessly with its leafy lair. Nature's own stealth mode!

850. Grab your hiking boots, explorers; we are searching for a fungus that hides its proper form by masquerading as a bird's nest! The bird's nest fungi are tiny mushrooms resembling nests filled with eggs! These fungi spread the spores to new locations with their "eggs" splashed out by raindrops. A clever dispersal strategy adapting to colonize new habitats!

851. From sea to sky, our next critter smells like garden fertilizer! The hoatzin bird, a native of the Amazon rainforest, is a flying fermenter. Its unique digestive system breaks down tough leaves, producing a manure-like aroma. It's a bird that's as intriguing as its scent!

852. Step into the mysterious stone buildings of Medieval Europe, where powdered mummies weren't just spooky; they were seen as healing wonders. Consumed for various ailments, this macabre medicine was a peculiar part of medieval health practices!

853. Wow! Look around, explorers; it's like we're in a field of jewels! Meet the mesmerizing amethyst deceiver, a small but regal mushroom. This mushroom is the fleeting jewel of the forest floor! Its vibrant color and transient beauty is a spectacular sight after the rain. A fungus with a gift for flare!

854. Get festive with the scarlet elf cup, a tiny, red, cup-shaped fungus! This medicinal gem of the woodland offers winter beauty and healing properties with its bright color. Its cup-shaped bodies are a beacon on the cold forest floor!

855. In Ancient Rome, around 100 CE, toothaches met their match with earthworm necklaces. Romans believed the natural vibrations of these wriggly creatures could soothe dental pain. A squiggly, slimy, but smart solution!

856. Zap back to Ancient Egypt, around 2750 BCE, where the locals had a shocking solution for aching muscles – electric eels! They believed these zappy creatures could stimulate healing, showcasing the Egyptians' innovative approach to medicine.

857. Mmmm! Taste the unique jabuticaba, a tree that bears its fruits directly on its trunk! This energy-saving trick allows animals to easily enjoy a snack and spread the seeds, its sweet and tart berries a beloved treat in its native Brazil! Nature's stealthy, yet selfless, snack bar!

858. Watch the shaggy mane mushroom turn into a black, inky substance! This shaggy spew of nature's drama offers a spectacle with its gills dripping black ink as it matures. A fungi whose cylindrical caps are a unique beauty in the meadow!

859. Grab your pinwheels, adventurers, and hold them to the wind! Our next fungus is named after this clever outdoor toy! The pinwheel mushroom is a tiny, delicate fungus with a unique structure! This spinning marvel of the forest floor offers a unique design with its cap supported by a thin stem attached to a central point; its delicate body is a lightweight wonder!

860. In Ancient Rome, tummy troubles found their match in crushed oyster shells. Romans believed these shelly substances could ease digestive woes. A crunchy cure from the markets of Rome!

861. Let's take a hike, but beware of the white baneberry with its striking, toxic berries! This plant ensures its long life and continued growth through the use of its toxic berries that look like small eyes. This fickle foe is excellent at deterring consumption and protecting its progeny. The white berry warning sign of North America!

862. Watch out, adventurers! Be cautious around the pitcher plant. It's quite the carnivorous trickster! This plant lures insects into its slippery pitcher with sweet nectar, a deadly trap leading to their eventual digestion. It is a sweet deception adapted to supplement its nutrient intake in poor soils!

863. Now, trotting across the Americas, meet the skunks! These black and white critters only spray their notorious scent when threatened by a curious dog or a wandering human. It's their way of saying, "Back off!" Remember, it's not personal; it's just skunky business!

864. Phew! Ahead, we'll explore the Himalayas for this peculiar stench. Here, the male musk deer is really making a name for itself! Its musk gland produces a scent sought after for centuries, contributing to some of the world's most opulent perfumes. A deer with a nose for luxury!

865. Now, let's wander through the sands to meet the timeless welwitschia, a desert dweller with only two leaves that it maintains throughout its millennium-long life! This plant is a living testament to life's resilience in the harshest conditions, drawing moisture from the foggy desert air to sustain itself!

866. Wow! Is that an underwater plant growing on the forest floor? The violet coral brings a pop of purple and underwater delight into the dark woods! This vibrant fungus is a showcase of nature's palette. The violet coral stands out with its bright, coral-like structure, its branching bodies a colorful inhabitant of the woodland floor!

867. Admire and be dazzled by the rainbow eucalyptus, nature's living art! Its multicolored bark peels away to reveal a stunning spectrum of hues beneath, a colorful display adapted to shed parasites and mosses!

868. Back on terra firma, the hawthorn shield bug stands at the ready in European gardens. This green and brown, shield-shaped bug releases a pungent scent when disturbed. Just a bug sporting aromatic armor!

869. Creep over to Ancient Greece, around 500 BCE, where snails weren't just garden dwellers but sore throat healers! The Greeks trusted in the soothing slime of snails to ease throat irritations – a slimy but ingenious solution!

870. Jetting off to Sweden, brace yourself for surströmming. Fished from the briny Baltic Sea, this small, silvery herring undergoes fermentation. The result? A true test for your nostrils. But for the brave, it's a taste of tradition. Dive in if you dare!

871. Phew! Ready to be blown away, junior botanists? Then hold your breath as we encounter the corpse flower, a towering giant with the scent of rotting flesh! This plant lures pollinators with its putrid perfume, a beacon of the truly bizarre in the plant kingdom. It blooms rarely and briefly, sometimes with years in between blooms!

872. Boo! Join me on a spooky exploration to meet the ghost orchid, a rare and leafless wonder! This plant lures the Sphinx moth with its sweet fragrance, its spooky white flowers seeming to float in mid-air, a phantom of the plant world relying on a specific fungus for its nutrients!

873. Quick! Plug your noses, everyone, and meet the rafflesia, the world's largest single flower! This parasitic marvel emits a foul odor to attract pollinators; its gigantic bloom is a rare and spectacular sight in the rainforests of Southeast Asia! A flower with a pungent power!

874. Hold your sniffers as we swim along to discover an aquatic aroma! Sargassum seaweed, floating in the Sargasso Sea, plays a vital role in providing a habitat for marine life. Its sulfurous song is a testament to nature's balance, offering shelter and food to countless ocean creatures.

875. Growing in the tranquil gardens of Ancient China, around 200 CE, moxibustion was a sizzling secret to pain relief. This technique was applied to relieve aches and pains using a spongy dried plant, a warm, soothing practice still used today!

876. Venture into the eerie world of Medieval and Renaissance Europe, where mummies found a second life in medicine cabinets! Ground-up mummy powder was a sought-after remedy for everything from headaches to stomach ailments – a macabre but popular medical ingredient!

877. Grab your gym shoes, explorers, because we've found a plant with a smell that competes! The Valerian plant, native to Europe and parts of Asia, is a tall, flowering herb. Its foot-like scent might not win fans, but its roots have been used for centuries as a remedy to help with sleep. Nature's own stinky lullaby, whisking you off to dreamland!

878. In Ancient Egypt, around 1550 BCE, a bald head called for a wild mix – crocodile, snake, and lion fat! Applied generously, this gooey concoction was the ancient answer to hair growth. Messy, yes, but a popular potion for those seeking luscious locks!

879. Hunt for the morel mushroom, a highly sought-after delicacy! This culinary masterpiece of the forest floor offers a unique flavor with its distinctive, honeycomb-like appearance. Its elusive presence is a forager's treasure!

880. Dress up and meet the veiled lady, an elegant mushroom with a lace formal dress! This graceful whisper of nature's design spreads the spores with its delicate skirt, its sleek appearance a unique sight in the tropical forests!

881. Do you feel that? It's the emotions of the sensitive plant or Mimosa pudica! Its leaves fold up at even the slightest touch, a botanical defense against predators that helps it protect its delicate foliage from harm!

882. From fish to cheese, we land in France. What's that smell? It's the Vieux Boulogne! This soft cheese, often enjoyed with a crusty baguette, has an aroma that might challenge your senses, but beneath that stinky exterior lies a pure gold flavor. A cheesy treasure waiting to be unearthed!

883. Admire the indigo milk cap, a fascinating, vibrant blue mushroom! This milky fungi offers a vibrant color and edibility. But here's a fun twist: Any damage inflicted on this mushroom causes a special blue liquid to release. This liquid is known as latex. Its blue caps are a colorful sight on the pine forest floor!

884. What's that smell? Phew! Hold your nose for the stinkhorn mushroom, a real stinker of the fungal world! This fungus spreads its spores with its unique scent, drawing admirers and detractors alike. A fungus with the most unusual spore dispersal technique!

885. Ready to be amazed, bewildered, and even a little disgusted? Then, come along to meet the Venus flytrap, a carnivorous marvel! This little warrior uses its hinged leaves to snap shut and ensnare unsuspecting insects, a survival strategy adopted in nutrient-poor soils where traditional photosynthesis isn't enough!

886. Be enchanted by the fairytale wonders of the fairy inkcap! This small, delicate mushroom covers hillsides, giving off the illusion of many resting fairies! It's a fleeting whisper of nature's artistry. A living fairytale whose delicate caps are a transient beauty in the grasslands!

887. Discover the Halfmens, a rare succulent with a thick, columnar trunk! This plant is said to be a half-human, half-plant creature turning to the sun, mourning its lost homeland. This plant also has a columnar shape, an adaptation to reduce water loss in the desert. A clever plant with a curious story surrounding it!

888. In Medieval Europe, around the 1300s, amidst the fear of the bubonic plague, sweet-smelling herb pouches were all the rage. Filled with fragrant herbs, they were carried around in hopes of warding off the dreaded disease. Fragrant, yes, but alas, not as effective as hoped!

889. Strike three, you're out! Let's adorn our baseball caps and admire the plant shaped like its name! The baseball plant, a round succulent from South Africa! This plant is a living reservoir in times of drought, its thick, fleshy walls storing water during periods of rainfall, a survival strategy in its arid homeland!

890. Look up, explorers, to see the dragon's blood tree, a multitasking marvel with an umbrella-shaped canopy! Its red sap, known as "dragon's blood," has been used for centuries as medicine and dye, offering shade and sustenance in its native lands!

891. Beware of the whimsical-looking but toxic fly agaric! This mushroom hides its potent effects behind its iconic appearance; its colorful cap of red or orange is a warning of the mysteries within. A storybook mushroom with a dark secret!

892. Hold your noses as we dive into Medieval Europe, circa 1300s, where swallowing wriggly, live fish known as cyprinids was the go-to remedy for stomach woes. A slippery yet surprisingly common cure in the medieval medical handbook!

893. In Ancient Egypt, around 3000 BCE, onion juice was more than a kitchen staple; it was a wound warrior! Applied to cuts and scrapes, it was believed to prevent infection – a tearful yet practical remedy from the sands of time!

894. Let's marvel at the monkey puzzle tree, but be careful; it's sharp! This uniquely named tree is an evergreen oddity from Chile and Argentina. Its branches look to be made of hundreds of monkey tales, and this living relic is thought to be quite ancient. Its sharp leaves and unique branches are a suspected adaptation to protect from herbivores of the past!

895. In Ancient India, around 1500 BCE, cow dung wasn't just for fields; it was a medical marvel! Used as an antiseptic dressing for wounds, this natural disinfectant was a cornerstone of Ayurvedic medicine. Unique and unexpectedly effective!

896. Let's slink by to meet the Eastern newt, found in the forests of North America. This slippery lizard releases a stinky, milky substance when threatened. These slimy secretions can irritate the skin of potential predators, ensuring the newt's safety. A slimy sign-off to our smelly safari!

897. Do you see that, scientists? Why, that's a mushroom lighting up the night! This bioluminescent fungus, the "Glow-in-the-Dark Mushroom," is quite a bright sight! They use this glow to their advantage by drawing in insects with their mesmerizing light. A nocturnal spectacle adapted to spread their spores upon the dark forest floor!

898. Watch the puffball mushroom release its spores! This fungus sends a cloud of spores into the air with a swift burst of pressure. Many of us have seen this powerful puffball, as its spherical bodies are common in meadows and woodlands. A smoky blast of new beginnings!

899. Prance through the forest to find the deer mushroom, an edible fungus with pinkish gills! This cervine-looking spectacle of the forest offers a unique color and spore production with its pink spores. It's a delicate cap of woodland delight!

900. Wading into North America's wetlands, what's that smell? Ah, it's the skunk cabbage! This leafy green plant, often found near streams, might remind you of old gym socks, but pollinating insects can't get enough. In the world of marshes, the stink is the star!

901. Prepare yourself for another stinky fungus as we discover the dog stinkhorn, a slim, cylindrical fungus with a pointed, smelly tip! This canine whisper of the fungal world spreads its spores with its foul-smelling, greenish-brown slime attracting flies, its slimy tip a beacon for the insects!

902. Trek through the lush Amazon rainforest, where the secretions of the Kambo tree frog were not just icky but incredibly useful. The indigenous people used it to boost their immune system and sharpen hunting skills – a testament to the rainforest's natural pharmacy!

903. Watch out; our next fungus is quite the invasive fellow! The transformed lobster mushroom is a parasitic fungus infecting other mushrooms! This nod to a seafood delicacy offers a unique flavor with its orange-red victims. It's a parasitic transformation, a gourmet chef's delight!

904. March into the Middle Ages, where crushed centipedes were all the rage for curing headaches. It's creepy and crawly, but these little critters were believed to pack a powerful pain-relieving punch!

905. Travel back to the Renaissance, around the 1500s, when lavender was used for its pleasant fragrance and as a remedy for headaches, insomnia, and even depression. A fragrantly fascinating insight into the herbal healing of the era!

906. Now, to our gardens, we trek in search of something pungent! Here, we might just find a brown marmorated stink bug. True to its title, it sends out a scent that's a clear "Back Off!" beacon to birds and other potential threats. This shield-shaped bug, often found in gardens and forests, has made its mark worldwide. Big smells come in small packages!

907. Grab your canoes, and let's float on the giant water lily, with its submerged stalk firmly anchored in the mud below; it's a true titan of the plant world! With leaves reaching up to 10 feet in diameter and strong enough to support a medium-sized animal, it's like a floating palace on the water's surface.

908. Be careful not to get enchanted by the enchanting spiral aloe! Its leaves unfurl in a hypnotic spiral, a living mandala whispering the secrets of nature's design, its geometric precision a stunning example of phyllotaxis in the plant kingdom!

909. Steer clear of the devil's tooth, a fungus with a twist! When cut, it oozes a dark red liquid similar to heparin, a blood-thinning medication, hinting at possible healing properties. With its tooth-like projections and eerie appearance, this fungus adds a touch of mystery to the forest floor, both spooky and potentially beneficial!

910. Watch out for the parasitic cordyceps! These clever invaders are taking over insects and arthropods! The parasitic cordyceps attach to and transform their hosts with their thread-like structures. They sit upon their host, continuing to grow and sprout. A clingy creature using its mind-controlling abilities to spark horror in the insect world!

911. Next, we gaze upon the earthstar fungi. These fungi reveal a spore sac with their outer layers splitting open, making it look like a tiny star's points! The shining star of the woodland floor!

912. In the vast landscapes of Ancient Africa, around 1000 BCE, termites were more than just wood munchers; they were stomach soothers! A brew made from crushed termites was believed to ease digestive issues – a crunchy yet common concoction for tummy relief!

913. Gobble gobble! Discover the turkey tail mushroom, quite the colorful fungus! This medicinal feat of nature's bounty offers health benefits with its layered, fan-shaped bodies resembling turkey tail feathers. A decomposer breaking down dead organic material!

914. Discover the lithops, or "Living Stones," nature's masters of camouflage! These plants blend in with stones to avoid being eaten, their leaf windows allowing sunlight to enter and photosynthesis to occur underground! This plant certainly rocks at blending in with its surroundings!

915. In the forests of Native America, around 1000 CE, willow tree bark was more than just tree skin; it was a natural painkiller. Rich in what we now know as aspirin, this bark was a testament to the deep-rooted wisdom of Native American healing practices!

916. Take cover as the sandbox tree, also known as the dynamite tree, launches its seeds! This tree ensures the survival of its progeny through explosive dispersal, its seeds flying through the air like tiny projectiles, a force of nature in the tropical rainforests!

917. Croak croak! Explorers, hear that sound? Let's splash into the ponds of North America and see what we find. It's the American bullfrog! This noisy amphibian also releases a musky scent when it's feeling threatened. It's a frog saying, "Give me some smelly space!"

918. The Humboldt squid is putting on a show deep in the Pacific Ocean. With its reddish hue, this giant, ten-armed squid releases a smelly ink when predators like sharks get too close. It's a dazzling display of defense in the deep blue, complete with a smelly ink finale!

919. Breathe in the aromatic world of Ancient Persia, around 500 BCE, where frankincense wasn't just for fragrance but for clearing congested chests. Inhaling its smoke was believed to relieve coughs and congestion – a sweet-scented solution for respiratory relief!

920. Now, we'll visit a creature not known for what it says but for how it smells! In the sandy dunes of North Africa, the fennec fox is marking its territory. This small, big-eared fox releases a musky scent to tell other animals, "This is my home!" It's this fox's clever way of drawing boundaries in the air!

921. Pew! Hold your noses while we observe the trapping techniques of the latticed stinkhorn. This red, bold, and cage-like fungus draws in insects for spore dispersal with its strong, unpleasant smell. A fungus whose cage-like structure is a beacon in the undergrowth!

922. Cheese lovers, assemble! In the heart of Europe, Limburger cheese is making waves. This soft, crumbly cheese, often spread on rye bread, has quite the footy fragrance. Aromatic echoes of flavorful tradition!

923. Let's head over to the beautiful islands of Hawaii to meet the unique cabbage on a stick! This plant is a singular treasure of the islands, its fleshy stem topped by a cluster of leaves resembling cabbage, a rare sight found only in specific island ecosystems!

924. Buzz back to Ancient Mesopotamia, around 3000 BCE, honey was the sweet solution to wound healing. Used as a natural antiseptic, this golden nectar was a common and effective remedy, showcasing the ancient wisdom of using nature's gifts for healing!

925. Drip, drip, drop! Rain on parched soil, a scent that's pure poetry. Surprisingly, Geosmin, a chemical produced by certain bacteria in the soil, is the maestro behind this earthy and very smelly encore. Nature's not-so-refreshing symphony!

926. Feel the sticky Sundew plant as it has set its deadly yet sweet trap! This carnivorous plant ensnares unwary insects in its sticky tentacles, a sweet embrace of doom, supplementing its diet in nutrient-poor environments!

927. Look to the sky, adventurers! Soaring high, the bearded vulture, a native of the high mountains from Spain to Tibet, might not be the freshest flyer. Its unique aroma results from its diet, consisting mainly of bones. It's a scent that says, "I've got a bone to pick with you."

928. Drift into the dreamy city-states of Ancient Babylon, around 1800 BCE, where sleep temples were the ultimate healing hubs. Here, dreams weren't just for night-time adventures; they were vital to curing ailments, with healers interpreting them to plan treatments. Dreamy and revolutionary!

929. But wait, plants have their own aromatic arsenal! The skunkweed, often found near the Mediterranean's coastal areas, is a small, unassuming plant. But disturb it, and it releases an aroma that's nature's own "No Trespassing" sign. A fragrant force field, if you will!

930. In Ancient India, around 1500 BCE, heated sandbags were not just for relaxation; they were a remedy for pain and discomfort. This warm and soothing technique, a precursor to our modern-day heat packs, was a clever and comforting approach to pain relief!

931. Be spooked by our next fungus, the dead man's fingers, a fungus resembling human fingers! This fungus releases spores to reproduce with its black, finger-like projections, a creepy showcase of life's continuation, its decaying appearance, a shout of renewal in the forest floor!

932. Stroll through Ancient China's serene landscapes, around 200 BCE, where a fever met its match with a unique concoction of crushed herbs and cold water. Applied with bamboo, this was one cool solution to turn down the heat of a fever!

933. In Ancient Greece, around 400 BCE, garlic was more than just a flavor enhancer; it was a breath of healthy air! This pungent bulb was a spicy, popular natural antibiotic used to treat respiratory ailments – a testament to the ancient Greeks' understanding of herbal remedies!

934. Grab your shovels! Let's dig deep to discover the Hydnora africana, a primarily underground parasite that looks much like a partially cut cantaloupe fruit! This plant lures insects into a deceptive pollination dance with its foul-smelling, flesh-colored flowers, a subterranean marvel relying on its host for sustenance!

935. In Ancient Greece and Rome, the mysterious mandrake root was more than just a plant; it was a potent anesthetic. Believed to induce sleep and dull pain, this magical root was a crucial player in ancient surgeries – a mystical yet practical remedy from the past!

936. Grow up, up, up! Let's get so tall with the sunflower as it tracks the sun across the sky! These flowers maximize sunlight exposure through heliotropism, their roots cleansing the soil of toxins, a purification dance adapted to thrive in contaminated soils!

937. What is that, hiding on the forest floor? It's the jelly ear fungus, a dark brown, ear-shaped delight! This culinary delicacy of the forest offers a unique ingredient in various dishes. It is well known for its rubbery, gelatinous texture and ear-like appearance, making this fungus a peculiar woodland treat!

938. Our next smell comes from a furry and sweet creature with a scent that can't be beaten! Ferrets, found across the Northern Hemisphere, are slinky little creatures with a musky scent. They use this scent to communicate, marking their territory and saying "Hello!" in their own unique way.

939. Let's venture into the rainforest to witness the walking palm, a fascinating tree with stilt-like roots! This tree is in a silent and steady race for life-giving light amidst the dense foliage, its roots allowing it to "walk" towards sunlight at a pace of 20 centimeters per year!

940. Careful! Beware of the devil's hand tree with its claw-like flowers! With its red, open, hand-shaped flowers and strong scent, this tree draws in bats for a nocturnal rendezvous. Its unique blooms are a striking sight in the forests of Mexico and Guatemala!

941. Let's stand in awe of the remarkable resurrection plant, a true survival artist of the plant world. It curls up into a tight ball during dry spells, conserving its energy and moisture. Then, with just a sprinkle of water, it miraculously returns to life, uncurling its leaves and turning lush and green again. This plant's ability to bounce back from the brink is a stunning display of resilience and adaptability.

942. If we go sniffing around the tropical rainforests of Central and South America, we'll find the lesser anteater is making a stink. When a jaguar or other predator gets too close, it releases a scent that could rival a skunk's, telling them to back off. It's a real champion of stink!

943. Say hello to a plant that is tiny but mighty! The wolffia is the world's smallest flowering plant! This plant hides its astonishing ability to spread and colonize, its minute size a rebellion against the conventional, floating freely on the water's surface! A minuscule flower that appears like slime on the water, neat!

944. Thousands of miles away lies our next spectacular stench. South Africa's milk of magnesia plant, found near streams and rivers, is a master of disguise. Its flowers mimic the look and smell of rotting meat to attract flies for pollination. A botanical bait-and-switch!

945. Grab a tall glass of water and take a sip with the bottle tree, a water-saving hero with a swollen trunk! This tree is a living oasis in arid landscapes, storing water to thrive in dry environments; its swollen trunk is a life-saving adaptation in its native Australia!

946. Let's walk the wooded paths and meet a fungi that looks like some leftover holiday decor. But this is no man-made object; it's the bioluminescent jack o'lantern mushroom! This lantern offers a breathtaking light show with its orange clusters glowing in the dark. Its toxic bodies are a warning sign on the forest floor!

CELESTIAL WONDERS & EARTHLY MARVELS

947. Grab your hiking gear, adventurers! We're headed to the Grand Canyon in Arizona! This colossal masterpiece spans a staggering 277 miles, unfolding before us with awe-inspiring trails and captivating vistas. It stands as a vibrant testament to the unparalleled artistry of the world.

948. Drive along the scenic trails of the Great Ocean Road in Australia! This picturesque route provides panoramic views of the limestone stacks known as the Twelve Apostles, magnificent rock formations that rise majestically from the Southern Ocean. It's a journey through nature's artistry, full of coastal beauty and the mesmerizing movement of the waves!

949. Experience the magic of the "Eternal Flame Falls" in New York. Nestled just behind a magnificent waterfall is a naturally occurring gas leak. This gas leak causes a flame to visibly burn behind the falls. The flame continues to burn for long periods and can easily be relit if extinguished. A true testimony that the world's hidden beauty can be found in the most unexpected places!

950. Did you hear that, ocean explorers? Oceanographers in 1997 sure did! One day, a mysterious sound echoed through the ocean, louder than any known creature. Named "The Bloop," its origin is still debated. Could this be an underwater whisper from the earth or perhaps a sea monster's call?

951. Dive deep into the ocean, where "black smokers" spew out mineral-rich water. These hydrothermal vents not only support unique ecosystems but might also hold clues to unlock ocean mysteries. Nature's underwater chimneys with stories to tell!

952. Now, let's dive deep into the vibrant underwater world of Australia's Great Barrier Reef! It's a bustling metropolis beneath the waves, home to over 1,500 species of fish and around 600 types of coral. It's a colorful symphony of life, whispering secrets of the hidden treasures beneath the waves!

953. Let's float along on the buoyant waters of the Dead Sea! With a salinity of over 30%, it's a unique sanctuary where you can float effortlessly in its salty embrace. This extraordinary body of water, lying at the lowest point on earth's surface, is rich in minerals beneficial for skin health. The high salt concentration means no marine life can thrive in it, making it a serene and otherworldly experience for swimmers.

954. Step into the surreal, geometric landscape of the Giant's Causeway in Northern Ireland! With around 40,000 interlocking basalt columns and hexagonal pillars formed by ancient volcanic fissure eruptions, it's like a stepping stone through geological time.

955. Light up the skies with lightning! This dazzling display of electricity lights up the thunderstorm, creating a symphony of light and sound known as thunder. It's a breathtaking ballet of energy and elements, illuminating the mysteries of the atmosphere!

956. Zoom through the skies with the jet stream! It's the fast-moving river of air at high altitudes, steering the dance of weather patterns and influencing the location of storms and temperature fluctuations. It's the invisible conductor of the weather symphony!

957. Dive deeper in the Red Sea, and you'll find "lakes" beneath the waves. However, something is amiss with these lakes or "brine pools," as they are almost completely uninhabitable! Only a few organisms, such as shrimp, worms, and bacteria, can inhabit these deadly pools. It's an oxygen-free oasis for only a few inhabitants!

958. Let's sail the winds with the Beaufort scale! It's a speedometer for wind, describing wind speeds based on observable effects on land and sea. It's a useful tool for anyone venturing into the elements, whispering the tales of the winds!

959. Behold the stunning spectacle of Iguazu Falls! Spanning 275 individual falls, this natural wonder is a breathtaking display of water in motion, boasting the most significant average annual flow of any waterfall in the world. It's a place where the waters roar and plunge, showcasing relentless power and mesmerizing beauty!

960. Wander through the timeless landscapes of the Namib Desert! It's known best for being the oldest desert in the world, telling tales of millennia under the sun. It also contains some of the world's driest areas. A place where the sands have seen it all, showcasing an ancient, unchanging world!

961. Time to grab our scuba gear once again to explore the Mediterranean Sea. The rising sea levels, and likely a combination of natural disasters, once hid an ancient Egyptian city beneath the waves. Thonis-Heracleion was a whispered leaf and was lost for over 1,200 years. However, this sea-claimed city was revealed in 2000, thanks to divers of the deep!

962. Feel the droplets on your skin? That's precipitation, nature's way of showering the earth with rain, snow, and hail! It's a magical dance of water droplets and ice crystals falling from the clouds to paint the world with different weather.

963. Let's explore the mysterious weather inversion! Imagine a blanket trapping warmth below and cold above. This phenomenon traps pollutants and helps create fog and temperature inversions, leading to a fascinating interplay of air and temperature layers, each with unique conditions!

964. Join me as we embark on a journey to the wonderland of the Galápagos Islands! These islands are like a living museum, hosting species found nowhere else, like the giant Galápagos tortoises and marine iguanas. It's where life has crafted unique masterpieces of diversity and survival!

965. Dance in the rains of the monsoons! Characterized by a shift in wind direction, they bring moist air from the ocean, resulting in a symphony of rainfall. They are the refreshing dancers of the weather world, bringing relief and whispering tales of flooding and challenges!

966. Feel the heat with heat waves! These are the long, sultry symphonies of high temperatures and humidity that affect health, agriculture, and infrastructure. They are the fiery dancers of the weather world, bringing the rhythm of drought and the melody of heat!

967. Can you imagine seeing the remains of an entire forest from yesteryear? The Underwater Forest is a cypress tree forest submerged and frozen in time. This prehistoric forest has been preserved off Alabama's coast for over 50,000 years. Nature's natural time capsule!

968. Don't let the "micro" fool you - the microburst is like a mini tornado within a thunderstorm. It can produce strong and damaging winds at the surface, posing a significant hazard to aircraft, structures, and trees. It's a powerful whisperer of the winds!

969. Let's climb aboard our deep sea submarine while we imagine a place deeper than Mount Everest is tall! The Mariana Trench is the world's deepest oceanic trench, plunging 36,070 feet. It's a realm where sunlight never reaches, and mysteries abound!

970. Peer down into the sea and discover a mountain range that dwarfs the Himalayas but is hidden beneath the waves! The Mid-Atlantic Ridge does just that, stretching over 10,000 miles. It's like earth has a twisting and turning underwater spine!

971. Feel the chill with the frost! When temperatures whisper below the freezing point, water vapor freezes into beautiful ice crystals, painting the world with a layer of frosty white. It's a delicate dance of ice and air, adding to the winter scenery and whispering tales of harm to the sensitive plants!

972. Let's visit the bubbling and steaming wonders of Yellowstone National Park! This park is like a giant outdoor science lab, with over 10,000 natural geysers, hot springs, and mud pots. The earth is making a steamy show, with the ground hissing and bubbling, telling us tales of what's deep beneath our feet!

973. Look up, fellow explorers! Clouds, the whimsical painters of the sky, are born when warm, moist air weaves water vapor into droplets or ice. With over 100 types, each cloud tells a different story of the skies!

974. Brace yourselves for the mighty tornadoes! These swirling columns of air descend from the thunderclouds, whispering winds of destruction. Their rapid rotation and high winds make them awe-inspiring yet frightening phenomena of the weather world!

975. Let's explore the magical Plitvice Lakes National Park in Croatia! Picture 16 sparkling lakes joined by a network of tumbling waterfalls and gentle cascades. It's like wandering through a watery wonderland, where each step reveals a new, glistening spectacle of nature's beauty.

976. Next, we take a journey to the lush and vital Amazon rainforest! It's the largest rainforest on earth and is like the green lung of our planet, producing a whopping 20% of our oxygen! A colossal sanctuary of life and biodiversity, it hosts an incredible range from jaguars and vibrant macaws to numerous indigenous tribes, all thriving in this majestic environment.

977. Ever wondered why cyclones spin? The Coriolis effect is a fascinating spin of the earth that swirls the air and fluids, creating whirlwinds and weather wonders in the Northern and Southern Hemispheres.

978. G'day mate! It's time to dive down under the waves as we explore the reefs of the land down under! Just imagine a canvas painted with every color imaginable. That's the Great Barrier Reef off Australia's coast, where over 2,900 individual reefs come together in a symphony of marine life!

979. Eyes to the oceans to see the hurricanes! These colossal storms bring winds and rains that dance and roar, causing storm surges and flooding. They are the titans of the weather world, with Category 5 being the most powerful.

980. Brace yourselves for the blizzard! It's a fierce snowstorm, a dance of winds and snowfall, reducing visibility and making travel a perilous adventure. It's a powerful force of nature, whispering tales of road closures and power outages!

981. Dive into the hydrologic cycle! It's the eternal dance of water between the earth and the atmosphere, involving stages like evaporation and precipitation. It's the planet's heartbeat, determining the rhythm of rainfall and the melody of weather patterns worldwide!

982. Soar above the towering elegance of Angel Falls in Venezuela! Its continuous drop of approximately 2,648 feet makes it the world's highest uninterrupted waterfall, a breathtaking cascade of grace and height. It's where the waters free-fall, untamed and beautiful, appearing to fall straight out of the sky!

983. Next, we're off to gaze at the reflective beauty of Salar de Uyuni in Bolivia! It's the world's largest salt flat, covering over 10,000 square kilometers. It transforms into a vast, natural mirror in the rainy season, creating an illusion where sky and land seamlessly converge on an endless horizon.

984. Venture into the frozen extremities of Antarctica's Dry Valleys! They are the driest places on earth, receiving as little as 2 mm of precipitation per year. It's a frozen feat of extremities, where the ice and wind create a display of the harsh, beautiful world at the edge of the earth!

985. Meet the barometer, the meteorologist's trusty sidekick! It's an instrument that measures atmospheric pressure, a critical factor in predicting weather changes. It's the silent predictor of storms and fair weather!

986. Help connect the puzzle pieces that lie just off Japan's coast! The Yonaguni Monument, an underwater formation, looks like a puzzle with curved edges and many layers. This intricate underwater wonder has sparked many debates! Is it nature's artwork or remnants of an ancient civilization?

987. Let's dive again into the mesmerizing depths of the Great Blue Hole in Belize! This underwater sinkhole, over 300 meters across and 125 meters deep, is a hidden gem of the deep blue. Around its edges, you might spot sharks, vibrant fish, and coral, making it a secret underwater world waiting to be explored!

988. Did you know there's only one place on earth where you can touch two continents at once? Welcome to Iceland's Silfra Fissure! Here, you can dive or snorkel between the North American and Eurasian tectonic plates. A rift where worlds literally collide!

989. Let's make our way into meteorology! It's the study of the atmosphere and weather where wise meteorologists use tools like weather balloons and satellites to unravel the secrets of the skies and predict the weather we experience daily.

990. Look, explorers! You don't want to miss it! The "Underwater Waterfall" (not far off Mauritius Island) is an optical illusion created by sand and silt deposits. This amazing marvel appears like a cascading waterfall on the ocean floor. One of the world's most breathtakingly beautiful natural wonders!

991. Is that a mirage in the distance? No, it's the vast and arid Sahara Desert! Spanning over 3.6 million square miles, it's the largest hot desert in the world. It's like a sea of golden sands.

992. Discover the not-so-hidden "Lost Blue Hole" in the Bahamas! This naturally occurring deep, circular hole on the ocean floor is a popular dive site! It is known for attracting a variety of marine life to its grassy edges, including seahorses, sharks, and juvenile fish! A lively mystery hidden beneath the waves!

993. Grab your climbing gear! We're scaling the staggering heights of Mount Everest! Nestled between Nepal and Tibet, it stands proudly at 29,032 feet and is the highest peak above sea level. It's a towering symbol of human aspiration, challenging all who dare to reach its summit!

994. Let's admire the thunderous beauty of Victoria Falls! With a width of over 1,700 meters and a height of around 108 meters, it presents a breathtaking display of cascading water and mist. Known as the largest waterfall in the world based on its combined width and height, Victoria Falls is a majestic testament to nature's grandeur.

995. Next, we explore weather fronts! These are the invisible lines where air masses of different temperatures and humidity clash, creating a symphony of weather changes and precipitation. They are the unseen warriors shaping the weather patterns of our world!

996. Discover the devastation left behind during WWII. The "Ghost Fleet of Chuuk Lagoon" in Micronesia is a graveyard of over 60 ships and 275 airplanes, sunk in 1944 and now a famous historical dive site. History that forever lies beneath the unforgiving ocean waves!

997. Is that a storm coming, miniature meteorologists? That means it's time to see rain shadows! They happen when moist air is pushed up over mountains and cools, leading to precipitation on one side and creating a drier and more arid environment on the other. It's the silent creator of deserts and lush lands!

998. Meet the twins of the climate world, El Niño and La Niña! They are the opposites of the Pacific Ocean, bringing warmth and chill to the equatorial waters and altering the dance of rainfall and temperature worldwide.

999. Discover Doppler radar! It's weather radar that assists in detecting and tracking precipitation and determining its type and intensity. It's the silent watcher of the skies, helping to identify severe weather events such as tornadoes!

1000. Let's venture into the desert to witness a haboob, an intense dust storm, or a sandstorm in arid regions. It forms when strong winds pick up and carry large amounts of sand or dust, reducing visibility and whispering tales of the treacherous desert winds!

1001. You're brilliant, future Einstein! You've daringly worked through 1001 facts and unlocked the doors to many fascinating mysteries! So keep asking, keep wondering, and keep learning. The world is an endless adventure, and you're the hero in your own incredible story!

TRIVIA TIME

1. When a hagfish feels threatened, how much can its slime expand?

2. What happens to a blobfish when it's brought from deep water to the surface?

3. How does the Eastern screech owl camouflage itself in North America?

4. Where is the walking leaf insect, which looks just like a leaf, mostly found?

5. What amazing thing can the triton snail do if it's injured?

6. Where does the violin beetle, known for its unique shape, usually live?

7. What clever trick does the ant-mimicking jumping spider use to avoid predators?

8. How do African bullfrogs survive dry periods?

9. How long have silverfish been around on Earth?

10. What sneaky thing does the Hairworm do to crickets and grasshoppers?

11. Why should you be careful around the small but mighty conga ant in Central and South America?

12. What does the Armadillo do when it's in danger?

13. How does the Sundew Plant catch bugs?

14. What sneaky way does the cuckoo bird use to make sure its babies are taken care of?

15. What makes the African bush viper both beautiful and scary?

16. Why is the venomous deathstalker scorpion being studied by scientists?

17. How does the Pygmy Whale escape predators?

18. What makes the manchineel tree, known as the "tree of death," both interesting and dangerous?

19. How far do monarch butterflies travel from North America to Mexico, and how many generations does this journey span?

20. When did the Cameroceras, a giant ancient cephalopod, live, and what marked the end of its era?

21. What special instinct leads green sea turtles to travel up to 1,400 miles for nesting?

22. When did the giant Diprotodon, a huge marsupial, go extinct?

23. What made the Baryonyx dinosaur a great fisherman in the Jurassic period?

24. Why is the Gasosaurus named so, and what's funny about its name?

25. When did the huge Short-faced Bear go extinct in North America?

26. How big were the eggs of the extinct elephant bird of Madagascar?

27. What made the Troodon possibly the smartest dinosaur, and what was unique about its brain?

28. How does the Tufted Deer hide when resting, and why?

29. What amazing skill do weaverbirds in Africa and Asia have?

30. How does a dolphin's echolocation help it hunt, and what is its hearing range?

31. Where is the Red-lipped Batfish found, and what does it do when resting?

32. How does the Red-lipped Batfish move on the ocean floor?

33. How do Red-knobbed hornbills in Indonesia protect their eggs?

34. What special role does the male Three-spined Stickleback Fish have?

35. How does the aye-aye lemur in Madagascar find and catch insects?

36. What are some cool adaptations camels have for living in the desert?

37. How much saliva do we make every day, and why is it important?

38. How much faster do our fingernails grow compared to our toenails?

39. What is eidetic memory, and how does it work?

40. How did the meningitis vaccine change the way we deal with the disease?

41. What do ancient 3.4 billion-year-old rocks tell us about early Earth?

42. How fast is a sneeze, and what does it do?

43. What cool thing do phages do against bacterial infections?

44. What kind of infections can Pseudomonas aeruginosa cause?

45. What amazing thing can marathon runners do, and what does it show?

46. What unusual thing did Ancient Romans use to wash clothes?

47. How was the Great Sausage Duel of 1865 between two German politicians settled?

48. What is the legendary city of El Dorado, and where is it supposed to be?

49. What important role did the tunnels and chambers of Naours, France, play in World War I?

50. What is La Tomatina, and where is it celebrated?

51. How heavy are the Moai statues on Easter Island, and who made them?

52. What was the Hoxne Hoard found in England, and what did it include?

53. Where is the Valley of the Kings, and which tomb is still undiscovered there?

54. What treasures were in the sunken Spanish galleon Atocha?

55. What's special about the Andean condor's flight, and how wide are its wings?

56. What special beak does the bar-tailed godwit have, and why is it helpful during migration?

57. How does the hammerhead shark's head shape help it hunt?

58. Where did the Medfly come from, and what damage does it cause?

59. How does the American alligator sense water ripples?

60. What's the top speed of a peregrine falcon when it dives for its prey?

61. Why did Australia introduce cane toads, and what was the unexpected result?

62. How do honeybees find their way back to their hive even on cloudy days?

63. What's unique about the northern snakehead fish in American lakes?

64. What did Ivan Pavlov demonstrate with dogs in the 1920s?

65. What's quantum teleportation, and how could it change the way we transmit data?

66. What unique teaching method did B.F. Skinner use with pigeons in the 1950s?

67. What natural ability of geckos is inspiring the development of new adhesives?

68. What causes echoes?

69. Who holds the record for the fastest human speed, and what was it?

70. What discovery about the brain's hemispheres did Roger Sperry make in the 1960s?

71. What fundamental structure within an atom did Ernest Rutherford discover?

72. How do our eyes function like cameras?

73. What were the first three animals to test a hot air balloon flight?

74. Who accidentally discovered saccharin, and how?

75. Which famous building gets struck by lightning about 23 times a year?

76. What was Roy Plunkett trying to make when he accidentally discovered Teflon?

77. What self-cleaning feature does the Sydney Opera House have?

78. How did Wilson Greatbatch invent the pacemaker by accident?

79. What's the length of the world's longest central span of any suspension bridge, and where is it located?

80. What's unique about the Bahrain World Trade Center?

81. What was William Perkin originally trying to make when he discovered the first synthetic dye?

82. What is the "King of Fruits" in Southeast Asia known for its potent aroma?

83. Which bird in the Amazon has a unique digestive system producing a manure-like aroma?

84. What's special about the bird's nest fungi and how does it spread its spores?

85. What did Ancient Romans believe could soothe toothaches?

86. What is unique about the jabuticaba fruit, and where is it native?

87. What's the defense mechanism of skunks?

88. What's the world's largest single flower and what's unusual about it?

89. What was the ancient remedy for stomach troubles in Greece and Rome?

90. Why is the Venus flytrap's trapping feature important?

91. What natural wonder in Arizona spans 277 miles with breathtaking trails and vistas?

92. What scenic route in Australia offers views of the Twelve Apostles?

93. Where can you find a flame burning behind a waterfall due to a natural gas leak in New York?

94. What is the mysterious underwater sound recorded in 1997, still debated today?

95. What are "black smokers" in the ocean known for?

96. Which sunken Egyptian city was revealed by divers in 2000?

97. What is the world's highest uninterrupted waterfall, located in Venezuela?

98. What underwater formation off Japan's coast has sparked debates about its origin?

99. Where can you snorkel between two tectonic plates?

SOLUTIONS

1. It can grow up to 10,000 times its original size!
2. It turns into a squishy, gooey mess.
3. Its feathers blend in perfectly with tree bark.
4. In the tropical forests of Southeast Asia.
5. It can regrow its shell and internal organs!
6. In the rainforests of Southeast Asia.
7. It acts like an ant to trick its enemies.
8. They make a cocoon out of mucus and shed skin.
9. Over 400 million years!
10. It controls their minds to make them jump into water.
11. It has a sting that feels like a sharp jab.
12. It curls up into a hard ball.
13. With its sticky leaves.
14. It lays its eggs in other birds' nests.
15. Its colorful scales and strong venom.
16. They're looking into its venom for medical uses.
17. It squirts out dark ink to confuse them.
18. It has apple-like fruits, but its sap can cause blisters.
19. They travel about 3,000 miles, and it takes four generations.
20. About 470 million years ago during the Ordovician period.
21. They return to the beach where they were born.
22. About 50,000 years ago.
23. It had a crocodile-like face and claws perfect for fishing.
24. It's named after the gas company that found it, making its name a bit funny.
25. About 11,000 years ago.
26. As big as a basketball!
27. It had a large brain for its size, making it super smart.
28. It sleeps with its head on its body, blending in with the forest.
29. They weave complex nests from grass and leaves.
30. Dolphins can hear ten times better than humans and use echolocation to find fish in the dark.

31. Near the Galápagos Islands, it hides in the sand.

32. It prefers walking with its unique fins.

33. The female seals herself and her eggs in the nest.

34. It builds nests and guards its young.

35. It taps on trees with its finger to find bugs under the bark.

36. Camels store fat in their humps, drink water fast, and keep sand out of their eyes and nose.

37. We make 1 to 1.5 liters of saliva daily for digesting food and fighting germs.

38. Three times faster.

39. It's like having a camera in your brain, remembering images and sounds in amazing detail.

40. It greatly reduced the threat of meningitis.

41. They show there were bacterial life forms back then.

42. A sneeze blasts air out at 100 miles per hour to get rid of dust and germs.

43. They fight harmful bacteria from the inside.

44. Various infections, especially in wounds and lungs.

45. They can run 26.2 miles in just over two hours, showing incredible human endurance and strength.

46. Urine, because it contains ammonia.

47. With a mock duel using sausages.

48. A city of gold, believed to be in Colombia's jungles.

49. They provided a safe place for soldiers and civilians.

50. It's a huge tomato fight in Spain's Bunol town.

51. They weigh up to 82 tons and were made by the Rapa Nui people.

52. A Roman treasure with coins, jewelry, and spoons.

53. In Egypt, and the tomb of Ramesses VIII is still missing.

54. Silver bars, gold coins, and emeralds.

55. It can glide without flapping, thanks to its 10-foot-wide wings.

56. Its beak senses air pressure changes, warning of storms during migration.

57. It broadens its vision and senses prey's electric pulses.

58. From Africa, damaging fruits and veggies around the world.

59. With special organs on its snout to detect the slightest movement in the water.

60. Over 240 miles per hour, making it the fastest animal on Earth!

61. They were brought in to control beetles, but they became an ecological problem by harming native wildlife.

62. They use the sun's rays and polarized light patterns to navigate.

63. It's a fierce predator from Asia that's upsetting the local ecosystem.

64. "Classical conditioning," where dogs learned to associate a bell with food.

65. It involves the instant transfer of information at a quantum level and could revolutionize data transmission.

66. Operant conditioning, teaching pigeons to play ping pong using treats and tricks.

67. Their ability to climb walls effortlessly.

68. Sound waves hitting a surface like a wall or mountain and bouncing back.

69. Usain Bolt, with a top speed of 27.8 mph.

70. Each hemisphere has unique talents: the left excels in logic and language, the right in creativity and intuition.

71. The atomic nucleus, where protons and neutrons reside.

72. They capture light and convert it into images we see.

73. A sheep, a duck, and a rooster, in 1783.

74. Constantin Fahlberg, after tasting something sweet on his fingers.

75. The Empire State Building in New York.

76. A new refrigerant.

77. Its roofs are covered with over 1 million glossy tiles that repel dirt.

78. By inserting the wrong resistor into a heart-rhythm recording device.

79. The Akashi Kaikyo Bridge in Japan.

80. It has integrated wind turbines for eco-friendly energy.

81. Quinine.

82. The durian fruit.

83. The hoatzin bird.

84. It resembles bird's nests with eggs, and raindrops splash out the spores.

85. Wearing earthworm necklaces.

86. It grows directly on the trunk and is native to Brazil.

87. They spray a notorious scent when threatened.

88. The rafflesia, known for its foul odor.

89. Crushed oyster shells.

90. To catch insects in nutrient-poor soils.

91. The Grand Canyon.

92. The Great Ocean Road.

93. The "Eternal Flame Falls."

94. "The Bloop."

95. Hydrothermal vents supporting unique ecosystems.

96. Thonis-Heracleion.

97. Angel Falls.

98. The Yonaguni Monument.

99. Iceland's Silfra Fissure.

UNTIL OUR NEXT EXPEDITION

You did it, fellow explorer! You sailed alongside me through 1001 facts, gathering a whole treasure chest of knowledge along the way. But remember, this journey is only the beginning of our many journeys together!

Always keep your compass of curiosity pointing true north, and never let your spark of wonder go out. Whether you're diving into the depths of the sea or scaling the greatest heights of your own magnificent imagination, there will always be more marvels to uncover.

Remember, gathering facts is only part of our journey. What truly matters is that we stay curious and never stop exploring the world around us. Every scientist, explorer, and visionary began as just a curious kid, much like you.

So, until we embark on our next grand adventure together, keep your mind curious and your heart filled with wonder. Our world is an endless quest of knowledge for those who seek it.

Until our next adventure,

Professor Prodigy

CERTIFICATE

OF ACHIEVEMENT

BEST AWARD

CONGRATULATIONS!

THIS CERTIFIES THAT

_____

HAS SUCCESSFULLY COMPLETED AN INCREDIBLE JOURNEY THROUGH

FASCINATING FACTS FOR CURIOUS KIDS

AND IS HEREBY RECOGNIZED AS AN

OFFICIAL EXPLORER OF KNOWLEDGE

AWARDED ON

_____

KEEP EXPLORING, STAY CURIOUS, AND REMEMBER THAT EVERY FACT YOU DISCOVER
IS A STEP TOWARD BECOMING A LIFELONG LEARNER AND ADVENTURER!

Professor Prodigy

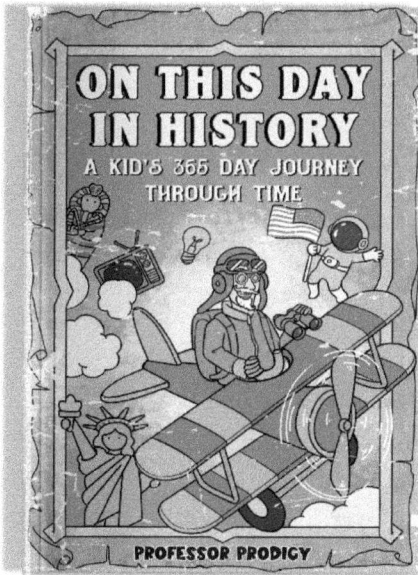

Get ready for Professor Prodigy's Next Adventure!

Coming 2024

Gear up to travel back in time with Professor Prodigy as he takes explorers on a new immersive learning adventure in "On This Day In History: A Kid's 365 Day Adventure Through Time" Each day will bring a new story, a fresh adventure, and a chance to explore the wonders of our world's past with Professor Prodigy. From the depths of ancient civilizations to the heights of modern marvels, get ready for a year-long journey that spans the sands of time.

Keep up with Professor Prodigy's Adventures

SCAN ME